## Other New and Natural Titles

Salads by Mary Norwak
Fruit by Pamela Westland
Herbs and Spices by Sonia Allison
Vegetables by Elizabeth Brand

# NEW & NATURAL

# Grains, Beans & Pulses

## Mary Norwak

BELL & HYMAN

First published 1985 by
Bell & Hyman Limited
Denmark House
37-39 Queen Elizabeth Street
London SE1 2QB

Cover design by Norman Reynolds
Illustrations by Paul Saunders

ISBN 0 7135 2525 8

**British Library Cataloguing in
Publication Data**
*Norwak, Mary
Grains, beans & pulses
1. Cookery (Cereals)
I. Title
641.6'31 TX808*

Typeset by Typecast Ltd., Maidstone.
Printed and bound in Great Britain at The Bath Press, Avon

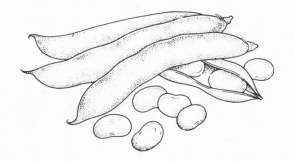

## CONTENTS

# INTRODUCTION

Grains and pulses are among our oldest and most natural foods. Millions of years ago, Man the Hunter augmented meagre flesh supplies with the seeds of grasses and podded plants, and later began to cultivate these plants around their primitive homes. In more recent history, families were glad of food which could be dried and stored to use during the hard winter months when fresh food was not available. The granary of an individual house or village was of vital importance to provide bread which has been truly called 'the staff of life'. Housewives found that dried beans and peas kept well and could be made into tasty soups and stews to provide nourishment and variety in the days before canning and freezing of fruit and vegetables became commonplace.

Sadly in recent times, these simple basic peasant foods have fallen into disfavour as increasing affluence and improved agriculture have provided huge quantities of meat, fish and dairy products to take their place. Even more recently however, medical evidence has shown that we need plenty of fibre and must avoid excessive animal fats, so that cereals and pulses are again being recognized as useful and attractive foods.

When this revival began, it was often thought odd and cranky to include pulses and grains in meals, apart from traditional rice and baked products. It was not always easy to find a variety of items, and they were often old and unappealing. Now grocers, health food shops and wholefood departments offer a wonderful range of fresh and beautifully presented foods, which are cheap and tempting. These pulses and grains can form a complete meal, for they complement each other to produce complete protein requirements (pulses alone are rich sources of protein, but mixed with cereal grains are a total substitute for animal protein).

This book aims to introduce cooks to the range of grains, beans and pulses which are now readily available. They are easily cooked ingredients and add variety and nourishment to every meal of the day and to every course of a meal. Even if one does not wish to give up meat altogether, one may make use of such ingredients to provide accompanying salads, tempting soups and first courses, unusual puddings and delicious cakes. Health may well be improved, and money will certainly be saved in a very pleasant way.

Just a word of warning, as pulses can be indigestible for some people and cause flatulence. Introduce them into the diet gradually and do not over-fill the family with bran and beans all at once, but make them a pleasant part of a meal, just like fresh fruit and vegetables until they are an accepted and attractive addition to a healthier diet.

Note: all recipes serve four people unless otherwise stated.

## *Acknowledgements*

The author and publishers would like to thank the following for the transparencies used in this book.

Allinson's Flour (facing page 24)
St. Lucia Products (facing page 25)
The Mushroom Growers' Association (facing page 48)
H. J. Heinz Company Limited (facing page 49)

# GLOSSARY OF GRAINS

## Barley

A very old food crop, but now mainly used for brewing. *Pot barley* is the complete grain with outer bran, and is the most nutritious form of the whole grain. *Pearl barley* is more widely available, and the oval cream-coloured grains are smooth and polished. *Barley flakes* are also available and also *barley flour* which has a distinctively sweet flavour. Barley flour is low in gluten-forming proteins and is not suitable for yeasted breads, unless mixed with wheat flour.

## Buckwheat

Not a true grain, but the seeds of a plant known as Saracen corn or wheat. It is very popular in Russian and Middle European cookery. The grain is normally roasted before cooking. *Buckwheat flour* is fine and dark with a strong savoury flavour, and is most often used in batters.

## Couscous

See Semolina.

## Maize (Sweetcorn)

Sweetcorn kernels may be cooked fresh on the cob, and are obtainable canned and frozen. Dried corn kernels may be heated until they explode to form popcorn. A variety of maize is ground to produce *cornmeal* which may be coarse or fine, and which is used for thickening, for puddings and soft breads.

## Millet

A very old food crop which is easy to grow and prolific, but which is only recently being recognized as a nourishing food in Europe. It has a high protein content and is richer in vitamins, minerals and fat than any other cereal. The husk is uneatable and this is removed for the saleable product which is easily digested in grain form or as flakes.

## Oats

A cereal which withstands a cold damp climate and which therefore features widely in Scottish cookery. The whole grain is known as a groat, and is rarely used as it takes a long time to cook. *Rolled oats* (sometimes known as *porridge oats*) are oat flakes produced by rolling the whole grain. *Jumbo oat flakes* are large and attractive in such mixtures as muesli. Oats are ground to produce *oatmeal* which may be coarse, medium or fine, and which is used for porridge and for baking.

## Rye

Another grain which flourishes in a cold climate and which is therefore used extensively in Russia, Scandinavia and many northern European countries. The flavour is rather sour, and this is most noticeable in the dark close breads made from *rye flour*. Rye flour is difficult to use in yeasted breads as it does not contain the right type of gluten-forming proteins. Rye flour may be mixed with wheat flour for baking, but a large quantity of raising agent is needed, and plenty of time must be allowed for dough to rise. *Rye flakes* are also available.

## Semolina

Meal ground from the endosperm or starchy part of the wheat grain, which may be coarse, medium or fine. It is most often used for thickening, for puddings, or for adding to biscuits to give crispness. Semolina made from hard (Durum) wheat is used for making pasta. Fine grains coated with flour are known as *couscous*.

## Wheat

This is the most commonly grown grain, and possibly the most widely used. The *wheat berry* or *wheat grain* contains all the nourishment of the cereal and it may be cooked to give a firm and filling grain. *Cracked* or *kibbled wheat* consists of the wheat berries crushed by rollers so that they cook quickly. This wheat is often used to give texture to bread either in the crumb or on the surface. When cracked wheat is hulled, steamed and roasted, it becomes *burghul* or *bulgur (bulgar)* and needs little cooking. *Wheat flakes* are similar, but have been rolled flatter and look like porridge oats.

When flour is milled from wheat, *bran* is produced, being the outer covering of the wheat grain, with a very high fibre content. *Wheatgerm* is the heart of the grain and contains most of the nutrients. These may be sold separately for use in recipes, or may be returned to the flour in varying proportions. *Wholemeal* or *wholewheat flour* contains the whole grain and may be stone-ground or roller-ground. *Wheatmeal flour* has had the wheatgerm and most of the bran removed to make it lighter. *White flour* has all the wheatgerm and bran removed.

# RICE

While a basic supply of long-grain and short-grain rice should always be in the store cupboard for savoury and sweet dishes, there are now many types available which can given variety to meals. White rice will keep for 18 months in a rigid container in a cool, dry place, but it is probably more convenient to buy small quantities of a number of different rices, some of which have a shorter shelf life.

When buying and cooking rice, it should be remembered that it swells considerably when cooked. 2oz (50g) uncooked rice will weigh 6-8oz (150-225g) when cooked, and this quantity is an average portion for 1 person.

## Boiling Rice

There is some vitamin loss when rice is boiled in water and it is wise only to use the amount of water which will be absorbed by the grain during cooking. Allow twice the volume of rice in water (e.g. 8oz (225g) rice to 1 pint (600ml) water), and bring the water to the boil. Stir in the rice and bring to the boil again, then cover and simmer until most of the water has been absorbed. Rice should be *al dente* and the easiest test is to hold a grain and insert the thumbnail which should just go in without resistance. Rinse the cooked rice in cold water and then in hot and tip on to a warm flat serving dish. Leave in a warm place or very low oven for a few minutes so that the grains steam-dry, moving them occasionally with a fork so that the grains dry evenly and are separate. Basmati rice cooks in 10 minutes; brown rice in about 30 minutes; all other types will be ready in 12-15 minutes.

## Steaming Rice

This is a favourite Chinese method of cooking rice, and is a little more complicated than boiling, but it produces a very light, fluffy texture. This is a good method for basmati and long-grain white rice, but brown rice takes a very long time. Boil a large saucepan of salted water and sprinkle in the rice. Stir well, bring to the boil and then stir again. Cover the pan, lower the heat and simmer for 5 minutes, then drain well. Rinse the rice in hot water and put it into a vegetable steamer. If the steamer has large holes, line it first with a piece of muslin, or aluminium foil in which fine holes have been pricked. Make several holes through the rice with the handle of a wooden spoon so that the steam circulates. Place the steamer on a pan of boiling water, making sure that the water does not touch the grains. Cover and steam for 45 minutes.

### Alternative Cooking Methods

Preparation in a *pressure cooker* will considerably reduce cooking time. Always check with the manufacturer's instructions to avoid mushiness. In a *slow-cooker,* rice may be left to cook at the lower temperature, and white rice will take 8 hours, but brown rice 10 hours. At the higher temperature, white rice will need 1 hour and brown rice 2 hours. The rice may be simply cooked in water, or in stock, or as part of a mixed dish. In the *microwave oven,* a few minutes will be saved when cooking rice, but it is probably more practical to prepare other items from the menu by this method, and leave the rice to cook reasonably quickly on the top of the stove.

# GLOSSARY OF RICE

### Long Grain Rice (Patna)

Long thin white grains of polished rice, which should be light, fluffy and separated when cooked.

### Short Grain Rice

### (Carolina or Pudding Rice)

Round short grains with a slightly chalky appearance, which become slightly sticky and cling together when cooked. Most often used for sweet puddings, the rice may be used for *risotto* or other savoury dishes in which the liquid is absorbed during cooking to produce a creamy result.

### Italian Rice (Risotto Rice, Arburio)

A short grain rice with slightly fatter grains, also known as *risotto rice* since it absorbs liquids and gives a creamy texture to that dish. *Arburio* rice from northern Italy has a particularly fine flavour.

### Basmati Rice (Pilau Rice)

Known as 'the prince of rices', this is a long grain rice of high quality and very good flavour. It does not stick when cooked and is the perfect accompaniment to Indian dishes.

### Brown Rice

Unpolished long grain rice with thin brown grains, which has a nutty flavour and chewy texture. It is more nutritious than white rice, but takes about twice as long to cook.

### Wild Rice

Not true rice but the seed of a wild grass. The seeds are long, thin and dark brown, turning slightly purple when cooked. Difficult to find and very expensive, but the perfect accompaniment to game.

### Easy-Cook Rice

Rice which has been part-cooked under steam pressure, which is then cooked in a carefully measured quantity of water. This rice may be packed loose in a box or sealed in a boil-in bag, and is light and fluffy when cooked. It is particularly easy to cook this rice in a covered casserole in the oven, which makes preparation easy for a large party without danger of over-cooking, or spillage of foaming water.

### Rice Flakes

Large irregular white flakes processed from rice grains which cook quickly to make soft-textured puddings.

### Ground Rice

Coarse ground grains which are usually cooked in milk to produce smooth and easily digestible puddings. Ground rice may also be used in tart fillings, and added to cakes and biscuits.

### Rice Flour

Finely ground flour made from grains. It is gluten-free and useful for those on low-gluten diets.

# GRAINS

## Muesli

Many muesli mixes are available, but this is a simple mixture which can be prepared according to taste and is not expensive.

*1lb (450g) rolled oats*
*1lb (450g) barley flakes or kernels, bran, wheatgerm, sesame and sunflower seeds (mixed to taste)*
*4oz (100g) chopped mixed nuts*
*4oz (100g) chopped dried apricots, apples, dates or figs*

1. Put the oats into a bowl and stir in the remaining ingredients until evenly mixed.
2. Store in an airtight container.
3. Serve with milk, cream or yoghurt, and sweeten if liked with brown sugar or honey. Add fresh fruit according to season.

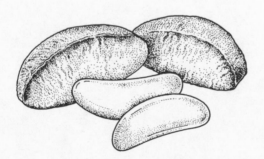

## Toasted Muesli

An unusual cereal with a delicious toasted flavour, which is good served with yoghurt or single cream and fresh soft fruit such as raspberries.

*1lb (450g) coarse oatmeal*
*3oz (75g) sunflower seeds*
*3oz (75g) cashew nuts*
*3oz (75g) desiccated coconut*
*3oz (75g) wheatgerm*
*3oz (75g) dark soft brown sugar*
*1½oz (40g) butter*
*1 tsp ground mixed spice*
*1 tsp salt*

1. Preheat oven to 160°C (325°F), gas mark 3. Spread the oatmeal on a baking sheet and bake for 20 minutes, stirring often.
2. Reduce heat to 150°C (300°F), gas mark 2. Stir sunflower seeds and nuts into the oatmeal and continue baking for 10 minutes.
3. Stir in the coconut and wheatgerm and continue baking for 15 minutes, stirring often to prevent burning.
4. Put into a basin while preparing the sweetening mixture.
5. Put sugar, butter, spice, salt and 2 tablespoons water into a thick small pan. Heat gently until the sugar has melted completely.
6. Stir into the oatmeal, mixing well. Leave until cold and store in an airtight container.

# Granola

This lightly toasted cereal has a deliciously nutty flavour and texture. It is served with milk, cream or yoghurt.

*1 muesli recipe (p.16)*
*8oz (225g) desiccated coconut*
*8oz (225g) vegetable margarine*
*8oz (225g) clear honey*

1. Put the muesli into a large bowl. Stir in the coconut.
2. Melt the margarine and honey over low heat. Stir into the dry ingredients and mix thoroughly.
3. Lightly grease a roasting tin. Sprinkle in the mixture but do not press down.
4. Bake at 190°C (375°F), gas mark 5 for 20 minutes, stirring frequently, until the mixture is evenly coloured and crisp.
5. Leave until cold. Store in an airtight container.

# Toasted Oat Cereal

A pleasant variation on the muesli theme which is good with milk or yoghurt. Other types of dried fruit or whole nuts may be added if liked.

*1lb (450g) jumbo oats*
*4oz (100g) sesame seeds*
*4oz (100g) wheatgerm*
*4oz (100g) skimmed milk powder*
*2oz (50g) sunflower seeds*
*2oz (50g) chopped mixed nuts*
*¼ pint (150ml) peanut oil*
*¼ pint (150ml) clear honey*
*8oz (225g) seedless raisins*

1. Mix together the oats, sesame seeds, wheatgerm, milk powder, sunflower seeds and nuts in a large bowl.
2. Put the oil and honey in a small pan and heat gently until runny and well mixed. Pour over dry ingredients and mix thoroughly.
3. Spread mixture on three large baking sheets. Bake at 190°C (375°F), gas mark 5 for 10 minutes, stirring once or twice.
4. Cool and stir in raisins. Store in an airtight container.

# Toasted Nut Cereal

Crunchy cereal mixture which is full of flavour and which is delicious served with milk or yoghurt.

*1lb (450g) rolled oats*
*2oz (50g) sunflower seeds*
*2oz (50g) hazelnuts*
*2oz (50g) almonds*
*2oz (50g) desiccated coconut*
*1oz (25g) sesame seeds*
*½oz (15g) wheatgerm*
*3 tbsps clear honey*
*3 tbsps sunflower oil*

1. Stir together the oats, sunflower seeds, chopped hazelnuts and almonds, coconut, sesame seeds and wheatgerm.
2. Mix the honey and oil and stir into the dry ingredients to blend well.
3. Spread on a lightly greased baking sheet. Bake at 180°C (350°F), gas mark 4 for 20 minutes, stirring frequently.
4. Cool and pack into a storage jar.

## Peanut Breakfast Cereal

A delicious change from processed cereals which is filling and tasty and which appeals to children. Serve with milk and some dried fruit if liked.

*8oz (225g) wholemeal flour*
*1oz (25g) wheatgerm*
*½ tsp salt*
*6oz (150g) peanut butter*
*¼ pint (150ml) water*

1. Preheat oven to 180°C (350°F), gas mark 4. Grease 2 baking sheets.
2. Stir together the flour, wheatgerm and salt. Mix the peanut butter with half the water and work into the dry ingredients. Add more water if necessary to make a soft but firm dough.
3. Divide the dough into 4 pieces. Put a piece of dough on to a sheet of baking parchment well sprinkled with wholemeal flour. Roll out gently to a rectangle about 12 x 9in (30 x 22.5cm).
4. Invert the dough on to a baking sheet and carefully peel off the baking parchment. Repeat with a second piece of dough on the other baking sheet.
5. Bake for 20 minutes until crisp and golden brown. Cool, break into pieces and store in an airtight container. Repeat with remaining dough.

N.B. If preferred, the dough may be cut into small shapes, e.g. stars or hearts with cutters before baking.

## Frumenty

A very old dish which is similar to porridge, but which was eaten on festival occasions with spices, cream and dried fruit, or even with a spoonful of brandy.

*8oz (225g) whole wheat*
*1½ pints (900ml) water*
*pinch of salt*
*1oz (25g) soft brown sugar, honey or black treacle*
*1 tsp ground allspice*
*3oz (75g) currants or seedless raisins*

1. Wash the wheat well and put into a casserole with the water.
2. Bring to the boil, cover and cook at 140°C (275°F), gas mark 1 for 4-5 hours until the wheat grains have burst and the mixture is like a thick jelly. This is the prepared frumenty which may be eaten plain with sweetening, milk or cream. Season lightly with salt before eating.
3. To make the dish more attractive, flavour the frumenty with sugar, honey or black treacle, spice and dried fruit. A little grated lemon rind or a spoonful of brandy may be added. Serve with cream.

## Russian Kasha

Buckwheat is a staple of the Russian kitchen and this dish may be served by itself or as an accompaniment to meat or fish. Minced meat or mushrooms cooked in butter may be folded into the cooked cereal, and soured cream is often added.

*2oz (50g) butter*
*1lb (450g) buckwheat*
*1½ pints (900ml) stock or water*
*salt*

1. Melt the butter in a thick pan and stir in the buckwheat. Cook for about 5 minutes over low heat, stirring all the time, until the buckwheat looks golden.
2. Add the boiling stock or water and salt.
3. Cover and bake at 180°C (350°F), gas mark 4 for 1 hour. Check the dish occasionally to see that the buckwheat does not burn, and add a little more liquid if necessary. When cooked, it should be tender, with the liquid completely absorbed.

## Breakfast Barley

A pleasant change from traditional porridge with a refreshing flavour of fruit, which may be served on its own or with milk or cream.

*½ pint (300ml) orange juice*
*½ pint (300ml) water*
*2oz (50g) dried apricots*
*pinch of ground cloves or cinnamon*
*4oz (100g) pearl barley*
*½oz (15g) butter or margarine*
*1oz (25g) chopped mixed nuts (optional)*

1. Put the orange juice and water into a pan. Add the apricots cut into small pieces, and the spice.
2. Bring to the boil and add the barley. Cover and simmer for about 1 hour until the barley is tender, adding more orange juice and/or water if necessary so that it does not become dry. The liquid should be absorbed when the barley is ready.
3. Stir in the butter or margarine, and the nuts if liked. Serve hot.

## Chicken with Couscous Stuffing

An original recipe with chicken breasts which livens up their rather bland flavour.

*1½oz (40g) couscous*
*¼ pint (150ml) boiling water*
*4 chicken breasts*
*3 tbsps soured cream*
*2 spring onions*
*1oz (25g) seedless raisins*
*pinch of ground ginger*
*pinch of salt*
*1½oz (40g) butter*
*1 tbsp oil*
*2 tbsps clear honey*
*1 tbsp soy sauce*

1. Put the couscous into a bowl and pour on the boiling water. Leave to stand for 5 minutes.
2. Put each chicken breast between 2 pieces of clingfilm or greaseproof paper and beat out until thin.
3. Stir the soured cream, finely chopped onions, raisins, ginger and salt into the couscous. Divide the mixture between the chicken breasts.
4. Fold in sides of chicken breasts over the filling and roll up to form parcels. Tie with cotton or fix with cocktail sticks.
5. Heat the butter and oil and fry the chicken rolls on all sides until golden. Cover and simmer for 15 minutes.
6. Mix the honey and soy sauce and stir into the pan. Cover and continue simmering for 5 minutes, occasionally spooning the pan juices over the chicken.

## Wild Rice and Mushroom Soup

Wild rice is extremely expensive but a little may be used to give flavour and texture to a clear mushroom soup.

*1½ pints (900ml) beef stock*
*1 small onion*
*1 small green pepper*
*1 tbsp chopped fresh parsley*
*1oz (25g) wild rice*
*4oz (100g) button mushrooms*
*5 tbsps red wine*
*salt and pepper*

1. Put the stock into a pan. Add finely chopped onion, pepper and parsley. Bring to the boil, cover and simmer for 15 minutes.
2. Wash the wild rice very thoroughly. Add to the stock, cover and simmer for 40 minutes.
3. Slice the mushrooms thinly and add to the soup with the wine. Season to taste. Cover and simmer for 15 minutes. Serve hot.

# Prawn and Millet Stir-Fry

A Chinese-style mixture of prawns and quickly cooked vegetables on a cereal base.

*4oz (100g) millet*
*3 spring onions*
*2 tbsps butter*
*¾ pint (450ml) chicken stock*
*2oz (50g) cashew nuts or peanuts*
*pepper*
*3 tbsps soy sauce*
*2 tsps cornflour*
*3 tbsps dry sherry*
*1 tsp sugar*
*¼ tsp ground ginger*
*¼ tsp paprika*
*2 tbsps oil*
*8oz (225g) peeled prawns*
*4oz (100g) button mushrooms*
*8oz (225g) mange-tout peas*

1. Mix the millet and finely sliced onions. Heat the butter and cook over low heat until golden.
2. Stir in the chicken stock and bring to the boil. Cover and simmer for 15 minutes. Remove from heat and stir in the nuts, and season with pepper. Place on serving dish and keep warm.
3. Stir together the soy sauce, cornflour, sherry, sugar, ginger and paprika and keep on one side.
4. Heat the oil in a heavy pan and add the prawns and sliced mushrooms. Toss over high heat for 4 minutes.
5. Stir in the soy sauce mixture and stir well until thick and bubbling. Add the mange-tout peas, cover and cook for 2 minutes. Pour into centre of millet mixture and serve at once.

# Cracked Wheat Burgers with Yoghurt Sauce

A variation on the solid meat burger with a tangy sauce. The burgers are best grilled, but they take on a very special flavour if cooked over a barbecue fire.

*2oz (50g) cracked wheat*
*1lb (450g) raw minced beef*
*1 egg*
*1 tbsp chopped fresh parsley*
*½ tsp mustard powder*
*¼ tsp salt*
*¼ tsp pepper*
*4 wholemeal baps or pitta breads*
*4 lettuce leaves*
*2 tbsps natural yoghurt*
*1 tbsp mayonnaise*
*pinch of ground coriander*
*1 small tomato*
*3 spring onions or 1 small onion*

1. Put the cracked wheat into a bowl. Cover with boiling water and leave to stand for 10 minutes. Drain well, squeezing out excess moisture.
2. Mix the wheat with the beef, egg, parsley, mustard, salt and pepper.
3. Shape into 4 round cakes. Grill under medium heat for 10 minutes.
4. Split the baps or pitta breads and put a lettuce leaf on the base of each. Put a burger on each lettuce leaf.
5. Stir together the yoghurt, mayonnaise and coriander. Skin and deseed the tomato and chop the flesh finely. Chop the onions finely. Mix into the yoghurt.
6. Spoon the sauce over the burgers and top with bread halves.

## Spanish Rice Omelette

A good supper dish which may be made from leftover rice, and which is just as good freshly made or cold. Use a large thick omelette pan for cooking.

*1 medium onion*
*1 green pepper*
*2oz (50g) butter*
*8oz (225g) cooked rice*
*2 tomatoes*
*8 eggs*
*6 tbsps milk*
*salt and pepper*
*4oz (100g) grated Cheddar cheese*

1. Chop the onion and pepper finely. Cook in half the butter over low heat until the onion is soft and golden.
2. Put the rice into a bowl. Skin the tomatoes and deseed them. Chop the flesh roughly and add to the rice.
3. Whisk the eggs and milk together and add to the rice. Mix well and season with salt and pepper.
4. Add remaining butter to the pan. Pour in the egg and rice mixture and stir well to mix in the onion and pepper.
5. Cook over very low heat for 15 minutes without stirring.
6. Sprinkle on the cheese. Remove from heat and cover the pan with a piece of foil, so that the omelette becomes firm.
7. Slice in wedges to serve.

## Corn and Crab Bake

A quickly made dish which makes a good supper. If crab is disliked, a mixture of flaked smoked haddock and peeled prawns is tasty.

*12oz (350g) corn kernels (fresh or frozen)*
*8oz (225g) crabmeat (fresh, frozen or canned)*
*3 hard-boiled eggs*
*2 tbsps lemon juice*
*1 tbsp chopped fresh parsley*
*½ pint (300ml) white sauce*
*1 tsp mustard powder*
*½ tsp Worcestershire sauce*
*2oz (50g) wholemeal breadcrumbs*
*1oz (25g) melted butter*
*1oz (25g) grated Parmesan cheese*

1. Cook the corn kernels until tender in boiling water (canned kernels need only be drained). Drain well.
2. Mix the corn, crabmeat, finely chopped eggs, lemon juice and parsley.
3. Mix in the white sauce and season with mustard powder and Worcestershire sauce.
4. Put the crab mixture into a greased ovenware dish. Mix the breadcrumbs, butter and cheese and sprinkle on top.
5. Bake at 180°C (350°F), gas mark 4 for 30 minutes. Serve with salad.

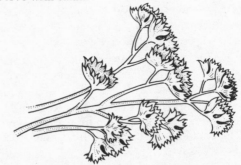

## Peppers with Brown Rice Stuffing

Brown rice gives flavour and a slightly nutty texture to this stuffing, which is also good in large tomatoes, courgettes, aubergines or marrows.

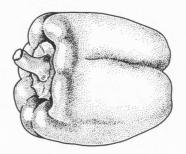

*4 green peppers*
*1 medium onion*
*1 garlic clove*
*2 tbsps oil*
*2oz (50g) brown rice*
*¾ pint (450ml) tomato juice*
*1 bay leaf*
*sprig of thyme*
*sprig of parsley*
*4oz (100g) chopped mixed nuts*
*salt and pepper*
*2oz (50g) grated Cheddar cheese*

1. Slice the tops from the peppers to form lids. Scoop out the seeds and membranes. Place the peppers in a greased casserole.
2. Chop the onion finely and crush the garlic. Put into a pan with the oil and cook over low heat until the onion is soft and golden.
3. Add the rice and half the tomato juice. Add the bay leaf, thyme and parsley. Cover and simmer for 40 minutes. Discard the bay leaf, thyme and parsley.
4. Mix in the nuts and season well.
5. Fill the peppers with the mixture and sprinkle with cheese. Replace the tops of the peppers. Pour the remaining tomato juice round the peppers.
6. Bake at 180°C (350°F), gas mark 4 for 35 minutes.

## Rice and Egg Cutlets

A simple supper dish which may be made from leftover rice. The cutlets are good served with a mushroom or tomato sauce and a green salad.

*3oz (75g) long grain rice*
*4 hard-boiled eggs*
*2 eggs*
*2oz (50g) softened butter*
*2oz (50g) grated Cheddar cheese*
*1 tbsp grated Parmesan cheese*
*salt and pepper*
*beaten egg*
*dried breadcrumbs*
*oil for frying*

1. Boil the rice in salted water for 12-15 minutes until tender but unbroken. Drain very well.
2. Chop the hard-boiled eggs finely and mix with the rice, beaten eggs, butter and cheeses. Season well with salt and pepper.
3. Form into flat cakes or cutlet shapes. Dip in beaten egg and breadcrumbs.
4. Fry in hot oil until crisp and golden on both sides. Serve hot with sauce.

# Corn Fritters

Crips puffy fritters which are good with chicken or ham, but may also be served with grated cheese or with mushroom or tomato sauce.

*4oz (100g) plain flour*
*pinch of salt*
*2 eggs, separated*
*2oz (50g) melted butter*
*3 tbsps milk*
*½oz (15g) sugar*
*8oz (225g) corn kernels*
*oil for deep frying*

1. Mix together the flour and salt.
2. Separate the eggs. Beat the yolks, butter, milk and sugar into the flour to make a firm batter.
3. If the corn is fresh or frozen, cook until tender and drain well. If canned corn is used, just drain well. Mix the corn into the batter.
4. Whisk the egg whites to stiff peaks and fold into the batter.
5. Drop spoonfuls of the batter into hot deep oil and fry until golden and puffy. Drain well and serve at once.

# Wholewheat Rolls

This dough has slightly more fat than most breads, which makes a rich dough which will keep well. A little more sugar may be added for a sweeter roll.

*1lb 5oz (600g) 100% wholemeal flour*
*1 tsp salt*
*1 tsp sugar*
*2oz (50g) vegetable fat or lard*
*1 sachet yeast*
*¾ pint (450ml) mixed milk and water*

1. Put flour, salt and sugar into a large warm bowl. Rub in the fat and stir in the yeast.
2. Warm the liquid to 43°C (110°F). Add to the flour and mix together by hand. Put on to a flat surface and knead for 10 minutes.
3. Shape into an even round shape and cover with the overturned mixing bowl or a piece of greased polythene. Leave to rest for 5 minutes.
4. Cut and weigh out dough in 2½oz (65g) pieces and shape into 16-18 balls. Put on a warm greased baking sheet, and cover loosely with polythene. Put into a warm draught-free area and leave for 35-40 minutes until approximately double in size.
5. Preheat oven to 220°C (425°F) gas mark 7. Bake for 10-15 minutes and cool on a wire rack. Rolls may be dusted with flour, poppy or caraway seeds, bran, crushed wheat or oats before baking for an attractive finish. A brushing with milk will give a rich colour; beaten egg will give a glossy shine; salted water a crusty finish

*Wholewheat Rolls (above)*

# Chicken with Rice Pilau

A richly flavoured dish of chicken and rice which may be conveniently cooked in one pan on top of the stove.

*3lb (1.35kg) chicken*
*1 garlic clove*
*2 tsp vinegar*
*salt and pepper*
*2 tbsp oil*
*5 tsp sugar*
*2 large onions*
*12oz (350g) long-grain rice*
*8oz (225g) canned tomatoes*
*1oz (25g) seedless raisins*
*1 whole hot chilli pepper (optional)*
*small bunch of chives*
*1 tbsp fresh thyme*
*12 green olives (optional)*
*1¼ pints (725ml) boiling water*

1. Cut the chicken into 6 or 8 pieces. Season with crushed garlic, vinegar, salt and pepper.
2. Heat oil in a large saucepan. Sprinkle in sugar and allow to brown. Brown chicken pieces in the pan.
3. Add sliced onions, rice, tomatoes and their juice, raisins, chilli pepper, chopped chives and thyme, olives and water.
4. Bring to the boil, cover and simmer gently for 25-30 minutes until the rice is tender and the liquid has been absorbed. Stir occasionally to prevent sticking.
5. Remove chilli pepper, and serve at once.

*Chicken with Rice Pilau (above)*

# Rice Loaf

An egg-stuffed savoury loaf which may be served with a hot tomato or cheese sauce.

*2oz (50g) long-grain rice*
*3oz (75g) shelled peas*
*3oz (75g) corn kernels*
*4oz (100g) mushrooms*
*1 medium onion*
*1oz (25g) butter*
*1 tbsp oil*
*1oz (25g) bran*
*1 tbsp tomato purée*
*1 tbsp soy sauce*
*2 eggs*
*salt and pepper*
*3 hard-boiled eggs*

1. Boil the rice in salted water for 12-15 minutes until tender. Drain well and reserve.
2. Cook the peas and corn in boiling salted water until tender, drain and mix with the rice.
3. Chop the mushrooms and onion finely and cook in the butter and oil until soft and golden. Mix with the rice.
4. Stir in the bran, tomato purée, soy sauce, beaten eggs and plenty of salt and pepper.
5. Grease and base-line a 1lb (450g) loaf tin. Put in half the mixture, and place the hard-boiled eggs in a line on top. Cover with the remaining rice mixture.
6. Cover with a piece of greased greaseproof paper. Bake at 190°C (375°F), gas mark 5 for 35 minutes.
7. Leave to stand for 5 minutes and turn on a warm serving dish.

# Cracked Wheat Pilaf

This quick pilaf made with cracked wheat (bulghur/burghul) may be flavoured with small pieces of vegetables and/or cooked meat or poultry. It makes a good accompaniment to casseroles and curries.

*2 tbsps oil*
*8oz (225g) cracked wheat*
*1 medium onion*
*1 garlic clove*
*1 pint (600ml) stock or water*
*salt and pepper*

1. Heat the oil and stir in the cracked wheat. Add finely chopped onion and crushed garlic. Toss over low heat until the onion is soft and golden.
2. Add boiling stock or water and season well.
3. Bring to the boil, then simmer for 30 minutes until the liquid has been absorbed and the wheat is tender.
4. Serve at once, stirring in small pieces of vegetable, meat or poultry if liked.

# Fruit and Nut Rice

This Middle Eastern version of risotto may be eaten on its own, but it is a good accompaniment for lamb, chicken or fish.

*1 medium onion*
*2 tbsps oil*
*8oz (225g) long grain rice*
*4oz (100g) dried fruit (raisins, sultanas, apricots, pears)*
*2oz (50g) walnuts*
*pinch of ground nutmeg*
*pinch of ground cinnamon*
*1 pint (600ml) stock*
*salt and pepper*

1. Chop the onion finely. Heat the oil and cook the onion until soft and golden.
2. Add the rice and dried fruit, chopping the larger pieces. Stir in the walnuts and spices.
3. Pour in boiling stock, stir well and season with salt and pepper.
4. Bring to the boil and simmer for 15 minutes, when the stock should have been absorbed.
5. Remove from the heat and cover the pan with a cloth and a lid. Leave to stand for 15 minutes so that moisture is absorbed and the rice becomes fluffy.

# Wheatgerm Stuffing

A tasty stuffing which may be used for poultry or fish, or for filling potatoes, peppers or rolled cabbage leaves.

*2oz (50g) wholemeal breadcrumbs*
*4 tbsps wheatgerm*
*1 medium onion*
*4oz (100g) mushrooms*
*1oz (25g) butter*
*2 tbsps chopped fresh parsley*
*2 tbsps fresh thyme*
*½ tsp fresh marjoram*
*1 tsp lemon juice*
*1 egg yolk*
*pinch of ground nutmeg*
*salt and pepper*
*water*

1. Stir the breadcrumbs and wheatgerm together.
2. Chop the onion and mushrooms finely. Cook them in the butter over low heat until soft and golden. Add to the breadcrumbs.
3. Stir in the herbs, lemon juice, egg yolk, nutmeg, salt, pepper and enough water to make a light crumbly stuffing. Use as required.

## Italian Risotto

The best rice to use for this dish is the Italian short-grain risotto rice, but brown rice is delicious too, although it will need longer cooking.

*1 medium onion*
*4 rashers streaky bacon*
*8oz (225g) mushrooms*
*2 tbsps olive oil*
*8oz (225g) risotto or brown rice*
*1 pint (600ml) stock*
*salt and pepper*
*4 tbsps grated Parmesan cheese*
*1 tbsp chopped fresh parsley*

1. Chop the onion, bacon and mushrooms.
2. Heat the oil and stir in the onion. Cook over low heat for 5 minutes. Stir in the bacon and continue cooking gently for 5 minutes. Add the mushrooms and cook for 1 minute, stirring well.
3. Add the rice and stir well until it is coated with the mixture in the pan.
4. Add boiling stock and season well. Bring to the boil, cover and simmer for 15 minutes until the rice is cooked and creamy (brown rice will need longer cooking, and more stock may be added so that the rice does not become dry).
5. Stir in the cheese and serve garnished with parsley.

## Barley and Mushroom Casserole

This casserole must be prepared the night before so that the barley swells and softens, and the result is delicious.

*1 medium onion*
*1 garlic clove*
*2 tbsps oil*
*8oz (225g) mushrooms*
*8oz (225g) pot barley*
*1 pint (600ml) stock*
*salt and pepper*
*1 bay leaf*
*2 tbsps grated Parmesan cheese*

1. Chop the onion finely and crush the garlic. Cook in the oil over low heat until soft and golden.
2. Slice the mushrooms and add to the onions. Continue cooking gently for 5 minutes.
3. Stir in the barley and cook for 1 minute, stirring well.
4. Pour in the boiling stock and season to taste.
5. Put the bay leaf in the bottom of a casserole and pour in the barley mixture. Cover and refrigerate overnight.
6. Bake at 190°C (375°F), gas mark 5 for 45 minutes. Remove lid and sprinkle with cheese. Continue baking for 10 minutes.

# Polenta

An Italian dish made from maize meal which may be served like a vegetable, and is traditionally eaten with game. It makes a good supper dish on its own with a tomato or mushroom sauce, or with plenty of grated cheese.

*2 pints (1.2l) water*
*8 oz (225g) coarse cornmeal*
*½ tsp ground nutmeg*
*salt and pepper*
*2oz (50g) butter*

1. Bring the water to the boil with a pinch of salt.
2. Sprinkle in the cornmeal and stir well. Simmer over low heat for 20 minutes, stirring occasionally. When the mixture is thick, season with nutmeg, salt and pepper, and stir in butter.
3. Place the mixture in a greased ovenware dish. Bake at 200°C (400°F), gas mark 6 for 25 minutes. Serve hot.

# Home-made Wholemeal Pasta

It is not difficult to make pasta, and the wholemeal variety is filling and full of flavour. Bread flour gives the best results.

*1lb (450g) wholemeal flour*
*1 tsp salt*
*4 eggs*
*2 tbsps olive oil*

1. Stir the flour and salt together in a large bowl and make a well in the centre.

2. Break in the eggs and add the oil. Gradually draw in the flour and work together to make a dough. Knead well for 5 minutes so that it becomes shiny and is no longer sticky.
3. Wrap in clingfilm or foil and leave to rest for 1 hour.
4. Roll out thinly on a lightly floured board. Cut into wide or narrow strips, separate and leave to dry slightly in the air for 1 hour.
5. Cook in boiling salted water, allowing about 8 minutes until tender but not soggy. Drain well and serve with butter and grated cheese, or with a sauce.

**4.** Place the tomatoes on a serving dish and fill with the cracked wheat mixture. Replace the 'lids' before serving.

## Tomatoes with Cracked Wheat Stuffing

A simple dish made with cracked wheat (burghul/bulghur) which is particularly good if made with the large fully-flavoured Beefeater or Marmande tomatoes.

*4oz (100g) cracked wheat*
*2 tbsps lemon juice*
*3 tbsps chopped fresh parsley or coriander*
*4 spring onions*
*4 tbsps olive oil*
*salt and pepper*
*4 large tomatoes*

**1.** Put the cracked wheat into a bowl and cover with cold water. Leave to stand for 1 hour, drain well and squeeze out surplus liquid.

**2.** Put the cracked wheat into a clean bowl and stir in the lemon juice and herbs. Chop the onions finely and stir in with the oil and plenty of salt and pepper. Leave to stand for 1 hour.

**3.** Remove the stalk from each tomato and turn them upside down on a plate. Slice off a 'lid' neatly and keep on one side. Take out the seeds with a teaspoon and discard. Up-end the tomatoes again and drain off surplus liquid.

## Cracked Wheat Salad

A favourite Middle Eastern dish made with cracked wheat, which is also sold as bulghur or burghul. Serve the salad with an accompaniment of natural yoghurt.

*8oz (225g) cracked wheat*
*2oz (50g) chopped fresh parsley*
*3 tbsps chopped fresh mint*
*1 medium onion or 4 spring onions*
*5 tbsps olive oil*
*5 tbsps lemon juice*
*salt and pepper*
*lettuce leaves*
*4 medium tomatoes*

**1.** Soak the wheat in cold water for 45 minutes. Drain well and squeeze out surplus moisture.

**2.** Mix with the parsley, mint and finely chopped onions.

**3.** Mix together the oil, lemon juice, salt and plenty of freshly-ground black pepper. Stir into the wheat mixture.

**4.** Arrange a bed of lettuce leaves in a serving dish and spoon in the salad.

**5.** Garnish with sliced tomatoes. If preferred, the tomatoes may be skinned and deseeded, chopped roughly and stirred into the salad.

## Brown Rice and Vegetable Salad

A colourful salad which makes a pleasant summer meal, or which may be served with meat, poultry or fish.

*1 medium onion*
*1 garlic clove*
*2oz (50g) butter*
*8oz (225g) long-grain brown rice*
*¾ pint (450ml) stock or water*
*1 tsp salt*
*½ tsp turmeric*
*8oz (225g) French beans*
*4oz (100g) shelled peas (fresh or frozen)*
*4oz (100g) corn kernels (fresh or frozen)*
*1 red pepper*
*4oz (100g) salted peanuts or cashew nuts*

1. Chop the onion finely and crush the garlic. Cook in the butter until soft and golden.
2. Stir in the rice until coated with the fat. Add the stock or water, salt and turmeric. Bring to the boil and then simmer for about 40 minutes until the rice is tender and the liquid has been absorbed.
3. While the rice is cooking, prepare the vegetables. Cut the beans into small chunks. Cook beans, peas and corn in boiling salted water until tender, and drain well.
4. Remove seeds and membrane from the pepper. Chop the flesh.
5. Cool the rice and vegetables and mix them together with the pepper.
6. Stir in half the nuts and place in a serving bowl. Sprinkle with remaining nuts. Serve with an oil and vinegar dressing if liked.

## Creamy Rice Pudding

Rice pudding should be cooked at low heat so that it is very creamy, and it is nicest when enriched with butter.

*2½oz (65g) pudding rice*
*2 pints (1.2l) creamy milk*
*2oz (50g) sugar*
*2oz (50g) butter*
*pinch of ground nutmeg*

1. Put the rice and half the milk into a greased pie dish and stir in the sugar and butter.
2. Bake at 140°C (275°F), gas mark 1 for 1 hour.
3. Stir in the remaining milk and continue cooking for 1 hour.
4. Stir again and sprinkle with nutmeg. Continue cooking for 1 hour.
5. Serve hot with cream.

# Rye Fritters

A quickly made treat for breakfast or teatime, or to use as an emergency sweet course. Sprinkle, with cinnamon-flavoured caster or icing sugar, or serve with maple syrup.

*4oz (100g) rye flour*
*4 tbsps baking powder*
*1 tbsp light soft brown sugar*
*½ tsp ground cinnamon*
*pinch of salt*
*1 egg*
*3 tbsps milk*
*1 tbsp oil*
*3oz (75g) seedless raisins*
*oil for deep frying*

1. Stir together the flour, baking powder, sugar, cinnamon and salt.
2. Beat together the egg, milk and oil and work into the dry ingredients, beating lightly until just mixed. Stir in the raisins.
3. Fry in deep hot oil until golden. Drain well and serve at once.

# Golden Rice

A rich and creamy rice pudding enhanced with marmalade, to be served with thick cream.

*1 pint (600ml) creamy milk*
*2oz (50g) short grain rice*
*3oz (75g) sugar*
*4oz (100g) coarse-cut marmalade*
*3oz (75g) unsalted butter*
*5 eggs*

1. Bring the milk to boiling point. Stir in the rice and simmer for 30 minutes until the rice is tender. Stir in 1oz (25g) sugar and put into a greased pie dish.
2. Spread lightly with the marmalade and hollow the centre slightly with a spoon.
3. Melt the butter and beat in the remaining sugar and then the egg yolks. Pour over the pudding.
4. Bake at 180°C (350°F), gas mark 4 for 30 minutes.

# Golden Honeycomb Pudding

A light variation on the steamed pudding theme which has an unusual texture and delicious flavour.

*¾ pint (450ml) creamy milk*
*6oz (150g) rolled oats*
*2oz (50g) light soft brown sugar*
*3 tbsps clear honey*
*1oz (25g) softened butter*
*1 lemon*
*pinch of ground cardamom*
*3 eggs*

1. Put the milk into a heavy pan and bring to the boil. Stir in the oats and cook gently for 5 minutes, stirring well.
2. Remove from the heat. Beat in the sugar, honey and butter. Add the grated rind and juice of the lemon, and the cardamom.
3. Separate the eggs and beat in the egg yolks.
4. Whisk the egg whites to stiff peaks. Fold into the oat mixture.
5. Put into a greased 2 pint (1.81 litre) pudding basin. Cover with greaseproof paper and foil. Steam for 1½ hours.
6. Turn out and serve with warm honey, golden syrup, custard or cream.

## Brown Rice Salad

A colourful salad with a variety of textures which is a useful dish for a buffet meal.

*4oz (100g) brown rice*
*pinch of salt*
*4oz (100g) shelled peas*
*4oz (100g) sweetcorn kernels*
*6 tbsps oil*
*3 tbsps wine vinegar*
*1 red pepper*
*1 small onion*
*2oz (50g) salted peanuts*
*pepper*

1. Put the rice into a pan of boiling salted water and boil for 20 minutes.
2. Add peas and sweetcorn and continue simmering for 10 minutes.
3. Drain well and put into a serving bowl.
4. Mix the oil and vinegar and pour over the warm rice mixture. Toss well and leave to cool.
5. Core and seed the pepper and cut the flesh in strips. Peel the onion and chop very finely. Add to the rice with the peanuts. Season to taste with pepper, and serve cold.

## Rice Fritters

Easily made fritters which are delicious served with melted jam or golden syrup. They may be prepared in advance and fried just before serving.

*4oz (100g) short grain rice*
*1 tbsp plain flour*
*4 egg yolks*
*2oz (50g) caster sugar*
*2 tsps grated lemon rind*
*pinch of ground cinnamon*
*2 egg whites*
*3 tbsps fine semolina*
*2oz (50g) butter*
*2 tbsps oil*

1. Boil the rice in salted water for 12-15 minutes until tender but unbroken. Drain very well.
2. Mix the rice, flour, egg yolks, sugar, lemon rind and cinnamon.
3. Form into 8 flat cakes. Dip in beaten egg whites and coat in semolina.
4. Heat the butter and oil in a frying pan. Fry the rice fritters on both sides until crisp and golden.
5. Serve very hot with warm apricot jam or golden syrup.

## Barley Pudding

A comforting winter pudding which is easy to digest and very nourishing.

*4oz (100g) pearl barley*
*1 pint (600ml) water*
*3oz (75g) seedless raisins*
*3 tbsps clear honey*
*½ pint (300ml) creamy milk*

1. Cover the barley with the water and bring to the boil. Simmer until the barley is soft, which will take about an hour, adding more water if necessary. The liquid should be completely absorbed when the barley is cooked.
2. Stir in the raisins, and honey and simmer for 5 minutes until the raisins are plump.
3. Stir in the milk, heat through and serve at once. If liked, flavour with a pinch of ground nutmeg or ground cinnamon.

## Italian Rice Cake

An almond-flavoured 'cake' which makes an excellent pudding to serve with apricot sauce or soft fruit, or just with whipped cream.

*6oz (150g) short grain rice*
*1 pint (600ml) milk*
*6 almond macaroons*
*4 eggs*
*1oz (25g) butter*
*1oz (25g) fine dry breadcrumbs*

1. Boil the rice in salted water for 3 minutes. Drain well and gradually add the milk, stirring well over low heat for 30 minutes until the rice is very soft and the milk has been absorbed. Leave until cold.
2. Crumble the macaroons into small pieces and add to the rice. Beat well and beat in 2 eggs and 2 egg yolks.
3. Whisk the remaining egg whites to stiff peaks and fold into the rice mixture.
4. Grease an 8in (20cm) loose-based cake tin generously with the butter and sprinkle the base and sides with the breadcrumbs.

5. Put in the rice mixture. Bake at 160°C (325°F), gas mark 3 for 40 minutes.
6. Leave in the tin for 10 minutes, then turn on to a warm serving dish.
7. Serve warm with sauce, fruit or cream.

## Barley Orange Pudding

An economical pudding which is light and nourishing. The flavour may be varied according to the type of marmalade used.

*1 pint (600ml) creamy milk*
*2 tbsps barley flour*
*1 tbsp light soft brown sugar*
*1 egg*
*3 tbsps orange marmalade*
*pinch of salt*
*pinch of ground nutmeg*

1. Mix a little of the milk with the barley flour to make a smooth paste.
2. Put the remaining milk into a pan with the sugar and heat to boiling point.
3. Pour on to the barley, stir well and return to the pan. Stir over low heat until boiling.
4. Cool for 10 minutes, then beat in the egg, marmalade and salt.
5. Put into a well-greased pie dish and sprinkle with nutmeg. Bake at 160°C (325°F), gas mark 3 for 30 minutes.
6. Serve hot with cream.

## Cracked Wheat Fruity Pudding

An easily made pudding which may be flavoured according to taste. It is very good served with yoghurt or cream.

*8oz (225g) cracked wheat*
*4oz (100g) dried fruit (raisins, sultanas, apricots,*
   *apples, pears)*
*1oz (25g) desiccated coconut*
*1 tsp grated lemon or orange rind*
*1 tsp sesame seeds*
*¼ tsp ground mixed spice*
*1oz (25g) light soft brown sugar*
*1 tbsp clear honey*
*1 pint (600ml) apple juice*

1. Put the cracked wheat into a bowl. Add the dried fruit, chopping the larger pieces.

2. Add the coconut, lemon or orange rind, sesame seeds and spice.

3. Mix the sugar, honey and apple juice. Pour over the dry ingredients and stir well.

4. Leave for about 2 hours until the wheat is soft.

5. Chill and serve with yoghurt or cream.

## Fruit Plate Pie

Apples may be used for a pie right through the year, but gooseberries, plums, cherries or apricots are delicious when in season.

*8oz (225g) 100% wholemeal plain flour*
*3oz (75g) hard margarine*
*1oz (25g) light soft brown sugar*
*2oz (50g) chopped mixed nuts*

Filling
*1lb (450g) cooking apples*
*2oz (50g) light soft brown sugar*
*1 lemon*
*½ tsp ground cinnamon or ginger*

1. Preheat oven to 220°C (425°F) gas mark 6. Grease a 9in (22.5cm) pie plate.

2. Put the flour into a bowl. Cut the margarine into small pieces and rub into the flour until the mixture is like coarse breadcrumbs. Stir in the sugar and nuts. Make a dough by adding cold water (6-10 tablespoons will be needed according to absorbency of flour). Shape the dough into a ball and chill for 30 minutes.

3. Roll out the pastry on a floured board and line the pie plate with half of it.

4. Peel and core the apples and slice them thinly. Place in the pie plate and sprinkle with sugar, grated rind and juice of the lemon, and the spice.

5. Cover with the remaining pastry and pinch edges together firmly. Bake for 25 minutes until crisp and golden.

# Raspberry Oat Creams

A rich but slightly sharp pudding which may be made well in advance and which has an unusual combination of flavours and textures.

*2oz (50g) medium oatmeal*
*4oz (100g) raspberries*
*¼ pint (150ml) double cream*
*¼ pint (150ml) natural yoghurt*
*1oz (25g) dark soft brown sugar*

1. Spread the oatmeal on a baking sheet and brown under a hot grill for about 2 minutes, stirring often until evenly coloured. Leave until cold.

2. Divide the raspberries between four individual dishes or glasses (the berries may be fresh or just thawed).

3. Whip the cream to soft peaks. Fold in the yoghurt until evenly mixed. Stir in the toasted oatmeal.

4. Spoon over the raspberries. Chill for 6 hours.

5. Just before serving, sprinkle with sugar.

# Derbyshire Oatcake

These oatcakes are big and floppy and are best eaten freshly made and hot. They may later be fried with bacon, or toasted to serve with butter or dripping.

*8oz (225g) fine oatmeal*
*8oz (225g) plain flour*
*pinch of salt*
*1oz (25g) fresh yeast or ½oz (15g) dried yeast*
*1 tsp sugar*
*½ pint (300ml) lukewarm water*

1. Stir together the oatmeal, flour and salt in a warm bowl.

2. Mix the yeast and sugar and add half the lukewarm water. Leave to stand until the yeast is frothing and bubbling.

3. Add to the dry ingredients and add remaining lukewarm water, beating well to form a thin batter.

4. Leave to stand in a warm place for 30 minutes until risen and bubbling.

5. Heat a griddle or thick frying pan and grease lightly. Pour a small cupful of the batter on to the hot pan and cook for 2 minutes. Turn and cook the other side. Serve hot.

# Rye Scones

These make a pleasant change from traditional scones, and are particularly good with cheese. Plenty of raising agent is needed for rye flour.

*8oz (225g) rye flour*
*3 tsps baking powder*
*1oz (25g) butter*
*1oz (25g) light soft brown sugar*
*¼ pint (150ml) milk*

1. Mix the rye flour and baking powder in a bowl and rub in the butter.

2. Stir in the sugar and mix to a soft dough with the milk.

3. Knead lightly and roll out 1in (2.5cm) thick. Cut into 2-3in (5-7.5cm) rounds. Put close together on a lightly greased baking sheet.

4. Bake at 230°C (450°F) gas mark 8 for 12 minutes. Cool on a wire rack.

## Oat Drop Scones

Textured soft scones which take little time to prepare. They may be lightly spread with butter or margarine and served with jam, honey or syrup.

*12 tbsps milk*
*3oz (75g) rolled oats*
*3oz (75g) fine oatmeal*
*1 tbsp light soft brown sugar*
*2 tsps baking powder*
*¼ tsp salt*
*2 eggs*
*1 tbsp oil*

1. Heat the milk to boiling point. Remove from the heat and stir in the oats. Leave to stand for 5 minutes.
2. Stir together oatmeal, sugar, baking powder and salt. Stir in the soaked oats and milk.
3. Separate the eggs and beat the yolks with the oil. Stir into the oat mixture.
4. Whisk the egg whites to stiff peaks and fold into the mixture.
5. Fry in spoonfuls on a hot greased griddle or thick frying pan, turning the scones when the surface bubbles to cook both sides evenly.
6. Wrap the scones in a clean tea cloth to keep warm and soft while all the mixture is cooked.

## Buckwheat Pancakes

This recipe should produce 8 large pancakes, which are delicious with maple syrup, honey or brown sugar and lemon juice.

*12oz (350g) buckwheat flour*
*4oz (100g) wholemeal plain flour*
*2oz (50g) wheatgerm*
*1oz (25g) light soft brown sugar*
*2 tsps baking powder*
*pinch of salt*
*2 eggs*
*3 tbsps salad oil*
*½ pint (300ml) milk or water*

1. Stir together the flours, wheatgerm, sugar and baking powder with a pinch of salt.
2. Mix the eggs and oil and stir into the dry ingredients. Add enough liquid to make a batter with the consistency of thick cream.
3. Grease a heavy frying pan and heat until the pan is hot. Pour in batter to cover the base thinly.
4. Cook gently until the surface is set and forming bubbly holes.
5. Turn the pancake and cook the underside until golden.
6. Keep hot while cooking the other pancakes.

## Wholemeal Pancakes

These pancakes have a spiced honey filling, but they may be served with jam, cream cheese, cooked dried fruit, or lemon juice and sugar.

*4oz (100g) wholemeal self-raising flour*
*pinch of salt*
*1 egg*
*½ pint (300ml) milk*
*oil for frying*

Filling
*2oz (50g) seedless raisins*
*4 tbsps clear honey*
*pinch of ground nutmeg*

1. Mix the flour and salt in a bowl. Make a well in the centre and add the egg and half the milk.
2. Beat well and gradually beat in the remaining milk to make a smooth batter.
3. Heat a little oil in an 8in (20cm) omelette pan. Pour in enough batter to coat the base thinly.
4. Cook until the pancake has set and the underside is golden brown. Turn with a palette knife and cook the other side.
5. Lift the pancake on to a plate and keep warm over a pan of hot water, covering the pancake with a clean cloth.
6. Repeat the process until all the batter has been used (this recipe should make 8 pancakes).
7. Mix the raisins, honey and nutmeg. Spread each pancake with some of the mixture and fold in quarters. Serve at once.

## Blini

These Russian pancakes are traditionally made with buckwheat flour, although a drier version may be made with half buckwheat and half wheat flour.

*12oz (350g) buckwheat flour*
*1 pint (600ml) milk*
*¾oz (20g) fresh yeast or 2 tsps dried yeast*
*3 eggs*
*4oz (100g) softened butter*
*½ tsp salt*

1. Put 3oz (75g) buckwheat flour into a warm bowl. Heat ¼ pint (150ml) milk until lukewarm and stir in the yeast. Add to the flour, cover and leave to rise in a warm place for 1 hour.
2. Separate the eggs. Cream the yolks with the butter and salt.
3. Add the yeast mixture and remaining flour and beat well until smooth. Cover and leave to stand in a warm place for 30 minutes.
4. Whisk egg whites to stiff peaks and fold into the batter.
5. Heat a griddle or thick frying pan and grease very lightly. Pour on batter to make pancakes about 3in (7.5cm) in diameter. Cook until the surface is lightly set and covered with bubbles. Turn and cook until golden on both sides.
6. Serve with caviar and soured cream, or yoghurt, or any smoked or salted fish.

## Irish Soda Bread

A textured loaf which needs no yeast and is quickly made. It should be eaten freshly baked and is delicious with unsalted butter.

*1lb (450g) 100% wholemeal plain flour*
*4oz (100g) fine oatmeal*
*1½ tsps cream of tartar*
*1 tsp bicarbonate of soda*
*½ tsp salt*
*1oz (25g) butter or margarine*
*¾ pint (450ml) milk and water*

1. Preheat oven to 230°C (450°C) gas mark 8. Grease a 9in (22.5cm) sandwich tin.

2. Stir the flour, oatmeal, cream of tartar, soda and salt in a bowl. Rub in the fat until the mixture is like breadcrumbs.

3. Stir in the milk and water to give a soft dough.

4. Put into the prepared tin. Bake for 15 minutes. Reduce heat to 180°C (350°F) gas mark 4 and continue baking for 20 minutes. Cool on a wire rack.

## Swedish Limpa Bread

A rich dark bread with a wonderful flavour of caraway seeds. Dried yeast does not work well with this loaf, which should be prepared with the fresh variety.

*7fl oz (200ml) brown ale*
*4oz (100g) black treacle*
*1 tbsp vinegar*
*1oz (25g) caraway seeds*
*½oz (15g) fresh yeast*
*1oz (25g) lard*
*8oz (225g) rye flour*
*8oz (225g) white bread flour*
*1 tsp salt*

1. Put the ale, treacle, vinegar and caraway seeds into a pan and heat slowly to lukewarm.

2. Crumble in the yeast and stir until dissolved. Add the lard cut in small pieces.

3. Put the rye flour into a bowl and pour on the hot liquid. Beat well.

4. Gradually beat in the white flour and salt and mix to a firm dough.

5. Knead lightly for 5 minutes until smooth. Put dough into a clean oiled bowl, cover with a cloth and leave in a warm place for about 3 hours until double in size.

6. Knead again, cover and leave to rise for 45 minutes until double in size.

7. Knead for 2 minutes until smooth and shaped into a round loaf. Put on a greased baking sheet and cover with a cloth. Leave to rise for 1 hour until double in size.

8. Bake at 190°C (375°F) gas mark 5 for 45 minutes. Cool on a wire rack.

# Barley Bannocks

Barley gives a sweet taste to breads and cakes, but these are always unyeasted as barley is low in gluten-forming proteins and does not rise well.

*1lb (450g) barley flour*
*4oz (100g) plain flour*
*2 tsps cream of tartar*
*½ tsp salt*
*½ pint (300ml) buttermilk*
*2 tsps bicarbonate of soda*

1. Stir together the flours, cream of tartar and salt.
2. Mix the buttermilk and soda until it fizzes and pour into the flour. Beat well to make a soft dough.
3. Roll out very lightly on a floured board ½in (1.25cm) thick. Cut into rounds the size of a tea plate.
4. Flour a hot griddle or thick frying pan, and put in a bannock. Cook over low heat until golden brown. Turn and brown the other side.
5. Serve freshly cooked with butter and honey.

# Oatmeal Soda Bread

A quick brown loaf which is delicious when freshly baked and served with salad or a light supper loaf. Try it too with a savoury spread or with chunky marmalade or honey.

*8oz (225g) wholemeal flour*
*6oz (150g) coarse oatmeal*
*2 tsps cream of tartar*
*1 tsp bicarbonate of soda*
*1 tsp salt*
*milk and water*

1. Stir together flour, oatmeal, cream of tartar, soda and salt.
2. Add enough milk and water to make a stiff dough. Work together until well mixed and form into a round loaf.
3. Place on a floured baking sheet and bake at 220°C (425°F) gas mark 7 for 25 minutes.

# Boston Brown Bread

This steamed bread may be cooked in pudding basins or stone jam jars, but it looks most attractive if cooked in clean food cans from which the tops have been removed (in this case, the tins must be wrapped in foil when the dough is put in before steaming).

*4oz (100g) rye flour*
*4oz (100g) cornmeal*
*4oz (100g) wholemeal flour*
*1 tsp salt*
*1 tsp bicarbonate of soda*
*6oz (150g) black treacle*
*¾ pint (450ml) buttermilk*
*4oz (100g) stoned raisins*

1. Grease 2 containers. Boil a large saucepan of water.
2. Stir together the rye flour, cornmeal and wholemeal flour with the salt and soda.
3. Add the treacle and milk and beat well. Stir in chopped raisins.
4. Fill the containers three-quarters full and cover with greased greaseproof paper and foil. Put into the pan so that water comes half way up the containers. Cover and simmer for 3 hours, topping up the pan with hot water occasionally.
5. Serve warm with butter. This bread is the traditional accompaniment to Boston Baked Beans.

## Rye Fruit Bread

This loaf may be eaten like a cake, or may be sliced and spread with butter.

*8oz (225g) rye flour*
*3 tsps baking powder*
*½ tsp ground cinnamon*
*½ tsp salt*
*4oz (100g) clear honey*
*1 egg*
*2 tbsps oil*
*7 tbsps milk*
*3oz (75g) seedless raisins*
*3oz (75g) chopped walnuts*

1. Preheat oven to 180°C (350°F) gas mark 4. Grease a 1lb (450g) loaf tin.
2. Stir together the flour, baking powder, cinnamon and salt.
3. Mix together the honey, egg, oil and milk.
4. Beat gradually into the dry ingredients. Stir in the raisins and walnuts.
5. Put the mixture into the prepared tin. Bake for 1 hour. Cool in the tin for 5 minutes, then cool on a wire rack.

## Spiced Cornbread

A quickly made bread which should be eaten when fresh and warm. It is a good accompaniment to bean dishes and to salads.

*4oz (100g) 100% wholemeal plain flour*
*4oz (100g) fine cornmeal*
*1 tbsp dark soft brown sugar*
*3 tsps baking powder*
*1 tsp salt*
*½ tsp ground coriander*
*8fl oz (225ml) milk*
*3 tbsps vegetable oil*
*1 egg*

1. Preheat oven to 190°C (375°F) gas mark 5. Grease a 1lb (450g) loaf tin.
2. Stir together the flour, cornmeal, sugar, baking powder, salt and coriander.
3. Beat together the milk, oil and egg. Add to the dry ingredients and beat well.
4. Put into the prepared tin. Bake for 30 minutes.
5. Leave in the tin for 5 minutes, then turn on to a wire rack to cool. Serve slightly warm.

## Pumpernickel

A dark close-textured loaf which is best sliced very thinly. It is excellent with cheese, oily fish or salted meats.

*2lb (900g) rye flour*
*2 tsps salt*
*1 pint (600ml) hand-hot water*
*4 tbsps black treacle*

1. If possible, use two 1lb (450g) food cans with one end removed, which have been thoroughly washed and dried (fruit or bean cans are excellent). If these are not available, use two 1lb (450g) pudding basins. Grease the containers well.

2. Mix the flour and salt. Add the water and black treacle and mix well. Add a little extra water if necessary to make a soft dough.

3. Divide the mixture between the containers, filling them three-quarters full. Cover with a piece of greaseproof paper and then foil, putting a pleat in the top to allow for expansion.

4. Put the containers in a saucepan and add boiling water to come half-way up the sides. Cover and simmer for 5 hours, adding more water if necessary so that the pan does not boil dry.

5. Turn out bread and cool on a wire rack. Leave until cold and then wrap in greaseproof paper and foil and store in the refrigerator.

## Corn Bread Crunch

A quickly made sweet bread which is good for breakfast or teatime, served with butter and honey or maple syrup.

*2oz (50g) cracked wheat*
*½ pint (300ml) boiling water*
*4oz (100g) coarse cornmeal*
*4oz (100g) plain flour*
*2oz (50g) rolled oats*
*2oz (50g) light soft brown sugar*
*3 tsps baking powder*
*½ tsp salt*
*2 eggs*
*9 tbsps milk*
*3oz (75g) chopped walnuts*
*2 tbsps maple syrup or clear honey*

1. Preheat oven to 200°C (400°F) gas mark 6. Grease a 9in (22.5cm) square cake tin.

2. Put the cracked wheat into a bowl and pour in the boiling water. Leave to stand for 10 minutes, drain and squeeze out excess moisture.

3. Stir together cornmeal, flour, oats, sugar, baking powder and salt.

4. Stir in the cracked wheat. Beat the eggs and milk together and work into the dry ingredients. Stir in the walnuts.

5. Spread the mixture in the cake tin. Sprinkle with the maple syrup or honey.

6. Bake for 20 minutes. Cut in squares and serve warm with butter or margarine, honey or maple syrup.

## Jumbo Date Flapjacks

Flapjacks are always popular but these are extra moist and spicy with the addition of dates.

*6oz (150g) vegetable margarine*
*4oz (100g) dark soft brown sugar*
*1 tbsp black treacle*
*8oz (225g) jumbo oats*
*8oz (225g) chopped dates*
*1 tsp ground mixed spice*

1. Preheat oven to 180°C (350°F) gas mark 4. Grease a Swiss roll tin.
2. Put the margarine, sugar and treacle in a thick pan and heat gently until the fat has melted, stirring well.
3. Stir in oats, dates and spice.
4. Press into the tin. Bake for 25 minutes.
5. Cool in tin for 15 minutes. Mark into squares or fingers with a sharp knife. Leave in tin until completely cold and then cut-into pieces.

## Caraway Barley Biscuits

Small sweet biscuits which are good with puddings or ices. If caraway flavour is not liked, use a pinch of ground nutmeg, cinnamon or ginger instead.

*2oz (50g) barley flour*
*2oz (50g) wholemeal self-raising flour*
*2oz (50g) light soft brown sugar*
*2oz (50g) butter*
*1 egg*
*1 tsp caraway seeds*

1. Preheat oven to 180°C (350°F) gas mark 4. Grease 2 baking sheets.
2. Stir together the flours.
3. Cream the sugar and butter until light and fluffy. Add the flour and beaten egg alternately to make a soft dough. Stir in caraway seeds or alternative flavouring.
4. Roll out thinly on a floured board and cut into shapes. Place on the prepared baking sheets.
5. Bake for 8 minutes. Lift carefully on to a wire rack to cool.

## Nutty Bran Fingers

Quickly made biscuits which are particularly useful for lunch boxes or picnics, but they are good with fruit or custard puddings too.

*6oz (150g) dark soft brown sugar*
*2 eggs*
*3oz (75g) wholemeal self-raising flour*
*pinch of salt*
*2oz (50g) All Bran cereal*
*2oz (50g) chopped walnuts or hazelnuts*
*4oz (100g) chopped dates*

1. Preheat oven to 180°C (350°F) gas mark 4. Grease and base-line a 7 x 11in (17.5 x 27.5cm) tin.
2. Beat the sugar and eggs together until light and fluffy.
3. Stir in the remaining ingredients and mix well.
4. Spread the mixture in the prepared tin. Bake for 30 minutes.
5. Cool in the tin for 10 minutes. Mark into squares or fingers with a sharp knife. Leave until cold and cut into pieces.

## Apricot Fingers

Biscuits which are full of flavour and texture to eat with a drink or to accompany a fruit or cream pudding.

*6oz (150g) rolled oats*
*4oz (100g) wholemeal plain flour*
*2oz (50g) wheatgerm*
*2oz (50g) soya flour*
*4oz (100g) dried apricots*
*4oz (100g) seedless raisins*
*2oz (50g) sunflower seeds*
*3 tbsps salad oil*
*2 tbsps clear honey*
*2 tbsps black treacle*
*4-5 tbsps orange juice*
*pinch of salt*

1. Preheat oven to 190°C (375°F) gas mark 5. Grease an 8in (20cm) square tin.

2. Stir together the oats, flour, wheatgerm and soya flour. Add finely chopped apricots, raisins and sunflower seeds.

3. Stir together the oil, honey and treacle and add to the dry ingredients. Add as much orange juice as is needed to make a soft but not runny mixture. Add the salt.

4. Place in the prepared tin. Bake for 25 minutes.

5. Cool in the tin, marking into fingers with a sharp knife while hot. Remove from tin when cold and store in an airtight container.

## Bran Banana Bars

Bananas give moisture and flavour to cake mixtures, and this spicy cake is delicious plain or topped with a cream cheese icing.

*6oz (150g) wholemeal flour*
*2oz (50g) bran*
*1½ tsps baking powder*
*¼ tsp ground allspice*
*¼ tsp salt*
*2 eggs*
*6oz (150g) light soft brown sugar*
*9 tbsps salad oil*
*½ tsp vanilla essence*
*3 medium bananas*
*3oz (75g) chopped walnuts*

Cream Cheese Icing
*3oz (75g) full fat soft cream cheese*
*2oz (50g) butter or margarine*
*½ tsp vanilla essence*
*12oz (350g) icing sugar*

1. Preheat oven to 180°C (350°F) gas mark 4. Grease a 11 x 7in (27.5 x 17.5cm) cake tin.

2. Stir together flour, bran, baking powder, spice and salt.

3. Beat together eggs, sugar, oil and vanilla until well mixed.

4. Mash the bananas and add to the egg mixture. Stir into the dry ingredients with the nuts.

5. Put into the prepared tin and bake for 30 minutes. Cool in the tin.

6. If liked, cut into squares to serve plain. To ice the cake, cream together the cheese and fat. Work in the vanilla essence and beat in the sugar until light and fluffy. Ice the cake, cut into squares and serve.

## Spiced Oatmeal Biscuits

Crisp biscuits which keep well in a tin and are good with a hot drink or with puddings or ices.

*8oz (225g) wholemeal plain flour*
*3oz (75g) medium oatmeal*
*3oz (75g) bran*
*5oz (125g) dark soft brown sugar*
*½ tsp ground ginger*
*½ tsp ground mixed spice*
*4oz (100g) vegetable margarine*
*¼ pint (150ml) cold water*

1. Preheat oven to 180°C (350°F) gas mark 4. Grease 3-4 baking sheets.
2. Mix the flour, oatmeal, bran, sugar and spices together in a bowl.
3. Rub in margarine until the mixture is like coarse breadcrumbs. Add enough water to make a stiff dough.
4. Roll out on a floured board ½in (1.25cm) thick. Cut in rounds 2-3in (5-7.5cm) across. Place on baking sheets.
5. Bake for 25 minutes. Lift carefully on to a wire rack to cool.

## Spiced Oat Biscuits

These are large crisp cookies which are easily made. They are good in a lunchbox, and delicious with tea or coffee.

*8oz (225g) light soft brown sugar*
*6oz (150g) butter or margarine*
*1 egg*
*2 tbsps golden syrup*
*1 tbsp water*
*½ tsp vanilla essence*
*4oz (100g) plain flour*
*1 tsp ground cinnamon*
*½ tsp salt*
*½ tsp bicarbonate of soda*
*8oz (225g) rolled oats*
*6oz (150g) seedless raisins*

1. Preheat oven to 180°C (350°F) gas mark 4. Grease two baking sheets.
2. Beat together the sugar and fat until soft and light. Beat in the egg, syrup, water and vanilla essence.
3. Sieve together the flour, cinnamon, salt and soda. Fold into the creamed mixture.
4. Mix in the oats and raisins.
5. Put tablespoonsful of the mixture well apart on the baking sheets. Bake for 15 minutes. Lift carefully on to a wire rack to cool.

# Health Crunch Cookies

The mixture of oats, wholemeal flour and dried fruit gives crisp little biscuits which are delicious with milk or a hot drink.

*4oz (100g) rolled oats*
*2oz (50g) wholemeal self-raising flour*
*2 tbsps wheatgerm*
*2½oz (65g) butter*
*4oz (100g) dark soft brown sugar*
*1 egg*
*½ tsp vanilla essence*
*3oz (75g) sultanas*
*3oz (75g) dried apricots*
*3oz (75g) chopped walnuts*

1. Preheat oven to 180°C (350°F) gas mark 4. Grease 3 baking sheets.

2. Stir together the oats, flour and wheatgerm.

3. Cream the butter and sugar until light and fluffy. Work in the egg and essence.

4. Gradually add the dry ingredients to the creamed mixture.

5. Fold in the sultanas, finely chopped dried apricots and walnuts.

6. Put teaspoonsful of the mixture on to prepared baking sheets. Bake for 15 minutes. Lift on to a wire rack to cool.

# Treacle Oatmeal Biscuits

Dark biscuits which are full of flavour and nourishment with added raisins and walnuts.

*6oz (150g) light soft brown sugar*
*4oz (100g) butter or margarine*
*4fl oz (100ml) black treacle*
*2 eggs*
*10oz (300g) wholemeal plain flour*
*1 tsp ground cinnamon*
*1 tsp salt*
*1 tsp bicarbonate of soda*
*12oz (350g) medium oatmeal*
*8oz (225g) seedless raisins*
*2oz (50g) chopped walnuts*

1. Preheat oven to 190°C (375°F) gas mark 5. Grease three baking sheets.

2. Beat together the sugar and fat until soft and light. Beat in the black treacle and eggs.

3. Stir together the flour, cinnamon, salt and soda until evenly mixed. Fold into the creamed mixture.

4. Stir in the oatmeal, raisins and walnuts and mix to a dough.

5. Form the mixture into about 20 balls. Place far apart on baking sheets. Dip a fork into cold water and press down the balls to flatten them lightly.

6. Bake for 10 minutes. Cool on baking sheets for 5 minutes, then lift carefully on to a wire rack to cool.

# Hiker's Snacks

Fruit-packed bars which give plenty of energy and are ideal for picnics or lunch boxes.

*3oz (75g) rolled oats*
*2oz (50g) demerara sugar*
*2oz (50g) chopped dates*
*2oz (50g) seedless raisins*
*2oz (50g) chopped hazel nuts*
*3oz (75g) black treacle*
*2oz (50g) hard margarine*

1. Preheat oven to 160°C (325°F) gas mark 3. Grease and base-line a 7in (17.5cm) square cake tin.
2. Mix together the oats, sugar, dates, raisins and nuts.
3. Melt the treacle and margarine and pour into the dry mixture. Mix well and press into the prepared tin.
4. Bake for 40 minutes. Cool in tin for 5 minutes and mark into fingers or squares. Finish cooling in the tin and cut into pieces before removing.

## Raisin Oatmeal Biscuits

Rough textured biscuits sweetened by raisins which are a pleasant contrast to fruit salads or ices.

*6oz (150g) light soft brown sugar*
*4oz (100g) butter or margarine*
*1 egg*
*4oz (100g) wholemeal plain flour*
*½ tsp salt*
*½ tsp bicarbonate of soda*
*½ tsp vanilla essence*
*9oz (250g) medium oatmeal*
*6oz (150g) seedless raisins*

1. Preheat oven to 180°C (350°F) gas mark 4. Grease two baking sheets.

2. Beat together the sugar and fat until soft and light. Beat in the egg.
3. Stir the flour, salt and soda together. Fold into the creamed mixture with the essence.
4. Stir in the oatmeal and raisins, and mix to a dough.
5. Form the mixture into about 15 balls. Place far apart on baking sheets. Dip a fork into cold water and press down the balls to flatten them lightly.
6. Bake for 15 minutes. Lift carefully on to a wire rack to cool.

## Oat Macaroons

A variation on the traditional almond macaroon which gives a pleasantly flavoured biscuit with a crunchy texture.

*3oz (75g) butter or margarine*
*3oz (75g) demerara sugar*
*2oz (50g) rolled oats*
*2oz (50g) ground almonds*
*½ tsp almond essence*
*2oz (50g) glacé cherries*
*1oz (25g) blanched almonds*

1. Preheat oven to 160°C (325°F) gas mark 3. Grease 3 baking sheets.
2. Cream the fat and sugar together and gradually work in the oats, almonds and essence to form a firm dough.
3. Shape the dough into pieces the size of a walnut. Put on to the baking sheets, allowing room to spread. Press down lightly with a fork dipped in cold water.
4. Cut the cherries into pieces and the almonds into strips. Put a piece of either cherry or almond on each biscuit.
5. Bake for 20 minutes. Cool on a wire rack.

## Savoury Oat Crisps

Cheese biscuits which are good to serve with drinks, or with soup or a salad.

*4oz (100g) rolled oats*
*4oz (100g) 100% wholemeal plain flour*
*4oz (100g) butter or hard margarine*
*4oz (100g) grated Cheddar cheese*
*1 tbsp grated Parmesan cheese*
*salt and cayenne pepper*

1. Preheat oven to 180°C (350°F) gas mark 4. Grease 3 baking sheets.
2. Stir together the oats and flour. Rub in the butter or margarine.
3. Stir in the cheeses and season well.
4. Form into a dough, adding a little water if necessary. Roll out thinly on a floured board and cut into rounds. Place on baking sheets.
5. Bake for 15 minutes. Leave on the tin for 5 minutes, then lift on to a wire rack to cool completely.

## Little Date Cookies

Small cakes with a crunchy pastry and sweet filling of fruit and nuts, which are delicious served with whipped cream.

*6oz (150g) 100% wholemeal plain flour*
*4oz (100g) rolled oats*
*5oz (125g) demerara sugar*
*3oz (75g) hard margarine*
*1 egg*
*½ tsp ground mixed spice*
*pinch of salt*

Filling
*8oz (225g) stoned dates*
*2oz (50g) demerara sugar*
*2oz (50g) chopped walnuts*
*¼ pint (150ml) water or orange juice*

1. Preheat oven to 190°C (375°F) gas mark 5. Grease 24 tartlet tins.
2. Stir the flour and oats together. Cream the sugar and margarine and work in the egg. Add the flour mixture with spice and salt and form into a dough.
3. Roll out carefully on a floured board and cut into 48 rounds. Line the tins with half the rounds.
4. Put the chopped dates, sugar, nuts, water or orange juice into a pan and heat gently, stirring until smooth. Leave until cold.
5. Fill the tartlet cases with the mixture and damp the edges. Cover with remaining pastry rounds. Brush with a little milk and make a small hole in the centre of each one.
6. Bake for 20 minutes. Leave in tins for 5 minutes and lift out carefully to finish cooling on a wire rack.

## Bran Buns

Little brown buns which are full of goodness, and which are particularly delicious at breakfast time.

*5oz (125g) 100% wholemeal plain flour*
*3oz (75g) bran*
*2 tbsps soya flour*
*2 tsps baking powder*
*pinch of salt*
*½ pint (300ml) natural yoghurt*
*2 eggs*
*2 tbsps clear honey*
*2 tbsps vegetable oil*

1. Preheat oven to 200°C (400°F) gas mark 6. Oil 18-24 bun tins.
2. Stir together the flour, bran, soya flour, baking powder and salt.
3. Gradually beat in the yoghurt, eggs, honey and oil. Beat well. The mixture should just drop from a spoon.
4. Half-fill the bun tins. Bake for 15 minutes. Cool on a wire rack.

## Spiced Wholemeal Shortbread

Nutty-flavoured shortbread with a hint of spices and lemon is delicious at teatime, but is also a good accompaniment to fruit and ices.

*6oz (150g) 100% wholemeal self-raising flour*
*1 tsp ground mixed spice*
*4oz (100g) butter*
*2oz (50g) light soft brown sugar*
*1oz (25g) ground hazelnuts*
*1 tsp grated lemon rind*

1. Preheat oven to 150°C (300°F) gas mark 2. Lightly grease two 7in (17.5cm) sandwich tins.
2. Put flour and spice into a bowl and rub in the butter until the mixture is like fine breadcrumbs.
3. Stir in sugar, nuts and lemon rind.
4. Press mixture into the prepared tins. Bake for 45 minutes.
5. Using a sharp knife, mark the shortbreads into 8 segments. Cool in tins for 10 minutes.
6. Turn on to a wire rack to cool. When cold, break into pieces.

*Bean and Mushroom Salad (page 77)*

*Overleaf: Bean and Vegetable Casserole (page 69)*

# Wholemeal Currant Cakes

These quickly made little cakes are light and delicious. Mixed dried fruit may be used, or sultanas or seedless raisins instead of currants.

*6oz (150g) 100% wholemeal self-raising flour*
*pinch of salt*
*4oz (100g) soft margarine*
*4oz (100g) light soft brown sugar*
*3oz (75g) currants*
*2 eggs*

1. Preheat oven to 200°C (400°F) gas mark 6. Oil 18-24 bun tins.
2. Put all the ingredients into a bowl and beat hard until light and creamy.
3. Half-fill the bun tins. Bake for 20 minutes. Cool on a wire rack.

# Ground Rice Cheesecakes

Tempting little tartlets for teatime in which the filling imitates the old-fashioned curd filling of traditional cheesecakes. A few currants may be added.

*8oz (225g) shortcrust pastry*
*3oz (75g) ground rice*
*3oz (75g) caster sugar*
*2oz (50g) butter*
*1 egg*
*2 tbsps lemon juice*

1. Preheat oven to 190°C (375°F) gas mark 5. Grease 24 tartlet tins.
2. Roll out the pastry and line the tartlet tins.

3. Mix together the rice and sugar. Melt the butter and stir in the rice mixture, beaten egg and lemon juice.
4. Fill the pastry cases three-quarters full with rice mixture.
5. Bake for 15-18 minutes until the pastry is crisp and the fillings risen and golden.
6. Lift carefully out of the tins and cool on a wire rack.

# Ginger Oatmeal Biscuits

Crisp plain biscuits which are richly flavoured and spiced.

*3oz (75g) fine oatmeal*
*3oz (75g) 100% wholemeal plain flour*
*2oz (50g) dark soft brown sugar*
*½ tsp bicarbonate of soda*
*½ tsp ground ginger*
*½ tsp ground cinnamon*
*¼ tsp ground mixed spice*
*3oz (75g) hard margarine*
*2oz (50g) black treacle*

1. Preheat oven to 160°C (325°F) gas mark 3. Grease 2 baking sheets.
2. Stir together oatmeal, flour and sugar with the soda and spices.
3. Melt the margarine and treacle together and cool. Mix with the dry ingredients.
4. Form the dough into small balls about the size of walnuts. Put well apart on baking sheets. Press down lightly with a fork dipped in cold water.
5. Bake for 20 minutes. Leave on the tin for 5 minutes, then lift on to a wire rack to cool completely and harden.

## Honey Bran Loaf

This teabread keeps well in a tin or may be frozen. Other dried fruit may be substituted for the dates.

*4oz (100g) clear honey*
*2oz (50g) light soft brown sugar*
*1 egg*
*½oz (15g) melted butter*
*4oz (100g) All Bran cereal*
*10oz (300g) plain flour*
*6oz (150g) chopped dates*
*2oz (50g) chopped walnuts*
*2 tsps baking powder*
*1 tsp salt*
*½ tsp bicarbonate of soda*
*12fl oz (350ml) milk*

1. Preheat oven to 180°C (350°F) gas mark 4. Grease and base-line a 2lb (900g) loaf tin.
2. Put honey, sugar, egg and butter into a bowl and beat well. Stir in the cereal.
3. Mix flour with chopped dates and walnuts, baking powder, salt and soda.
4. Add the flour to the bran mixture alternately with the milk. Stir well but do not over-beat.
5. Put into the prepared tin. Bake for 1¼ hours. Cool in the tin before turning out.
6. Serve in slices, with butter if liked.

## Wholemeal Victoria Sandwich

The refreshing filling of this sponge sandwich nicely offsets the rich flavour of the golden-brown cake. Chopped dried apricots or dates may be added to the filling for a special occasion.

*6oz (150g) soft margarine*
*6oz (150g) light soft brown sugar*
*3 eggs*
*6oz (150g) 100% wholemeal self-raising flour*

Filling
*8oz (225g) curd cheese*
*3 tsps clear honey*
*pinch of ground ginger or cinnamon*

1. Preheat oven to 190°C (375°F) gas mark 5. Grease and base-line two 7in (17.5cm) sandwich tins.
2. Put all the ingredients into a bowl and beat hard until light and fluffy (if using a food processor, add 1½ teaspoons baking powder).
3. Divide mixture between the tins. Bake for 25 minutes.
4. Leave in the tins for 5 minutes, then turn on to a wire rack to cool.
5. To make the filling, cream the cheese, honey and spice together. Sandwich the cakes together with half the filling. Spread the remaining filling on top of the cake. If liked, sprinkle with some chopped mixed nuts.

# Nutty Bran Loaf

This makes a pleasant cake, or the slices may be buttered, or spread with honey.

*6oz (150g) wheatmeal self-raising flour*
*1oz (25g) bran*
*1 tsp bicarbonate of soda*
*½ tsp ground mixed spice*
*pinch of salt*
*4oz (100g) dark soft brown sugar*
*4oz (100g) chopped walnuts or hazelnuts*
*¼ pint (150ml) natural yoghurt*
*4 tbsps vegetable oil*
*1 egg*
*2 tsps grated orange rind*

1. Preheat oven to 190°C (375°F) gas mark 5. Grease and base-line a 1½lb (675g) loaf tin.
2. Stir together the flour, bran, soda, spice, salt, sugar and nuts.
3. Beat together the yoghurt, oil, egg and orange rind. Add to the dry ingredients and beat well.
4. Bake for 1¼ hours. Cool in the tin for 10 minutes, then turn on to a wire rack to finish cooling.

# Barley Harvest Cake

A plain cake with a pleasantly sweet taste which is good at teatime, but makes a nice finish to a picnic.

*8oz (225g) barley flour*
*8oz (225g) plain flour*
*1½ tsps baking powder*
*½ tsp salt*
*4oz (100g) butter*
*4oz (100g) light soft brown sugar*
*½ pint (300ml) milk*
*8oz (225g) sultanas*

1. Preheat oven to 180°C (350°F) gas mark 4. Grease and base-line a 7in (17.5cm) round cake tin.
2. Stir together the flours, baking powder and salt.
3. Cream the butter and sugar until light and fluffy.
4. Add the dry ingredients and milk alternately, beating between each addition. Fold in the sultanas.
5. Put into the prepared tin and bake for 1½ hours.
6. Cool in the tin for 10 minutes, then finish cooling on a wire rack.

# Apple Muesli Cake

A good family cake which keeps well in a tin and which needs no icing or filling.

*6oz (150g) muesli*
*6oz (150g) mixed dried fruit*
*4oz (100g) dark soft brown sugar*
*2 tbsps malt extract*
*½ pint (300ml) apple juice*
*7oz (175g) wholemeal plain flour*
*3 tsps baking powder*
*2 eating apples*
*2oz (50g) chopped walnuts*

1. Put the muesli, fruit, sugar and malt extract in a bowl and add the apple juice. Stir well and leave to stand for 30 minutes.
2. Preheat oven to 180°C (350°F) gas mark 4. Grease and base-line a 7in (17.5cm) round cake tin.
3. Stir the flour and baking powder together and mix into the soaked muesli.
4. Peel and core the apples. Grate them coarsely and add to the cake mixture with the walnuts.
5. Put into the prepared tin. Bake for 1 hour 45 minutes. Leave to cool in tin for 10 minutes, then turn out on a wire rack to finish cooling.

## Carrot and Almond Cake

A simple cake flavoured and sweetened by carrots has a subtle almond flavour. It needs no decoration, but some demerara sugar and chopped nuts may be sprinkled on before baking to give a crunchy finish.

*8oz (225g) 81% wholemeal plain flour*
*8oz (225g) soft margarine*
*8oz (225g) light soft brown sugar*
*4oz (100g) ground almonds*
*4 eggs*
*8oz (225g) grated raw carrots*
*1 lemon*

1. Preheat oven to 180°C (350°F) gas mark 4. Grease and base-line a 7in (17.5cm) round cake tin.
2. Put the flour, margarine, sugar, almonds and eggs into a bowl. Beat hard until the mixture is light and soft.
3. Beat in the carrots and the grated rind and juice of the lemon.
4. Put into the prepared tin. Bake for 1½ hours.
5. Cool in the tin for 10 minutes, then turn on to a wire rack to cool.

## Ginger Parkin

A traditional gingerbread which is best if stored in a tin for three or four days before cutting. It is very good eaten with a piece of farmhouse cheese.

*4oz (100g) wholemeal plain flour*
*12oz (350g) medium oatmeal*
*1 tsp ground ginger*
*4oz (100g) butter or margarine*
*4oz (100g) black treacle*
*4oz (100g) honey*
*4 tbsps milk*
*½ tsp bicarbonate of soda*

1. Preheat oven to 160°C (325°F) gas mark 3. Grease and base-line a 7 x 11in (17.5 x 27.5cm) tin.
2. Stir the flour, oatmeal and ginger together in a bowl until evenly coloured.
3. Put the fat, treacle and honey into a pan and heat gently until the fat has melted. Pour into the dry ingredients and beat well.
4. Heat the milk to lukewarm. Stir in the soda and add to the cake mixture. Beat well and pour into the tin.
5. Bake for 1½ hours. Cool in the tin for 10 minutes, then turn on to a wire rack to cool. Store in an airtight tin.

## Lemon Barley Water

An old-fashioned drink which is very refreshing in hot weather. It is also nourishing and digestible for invalids.

*3oz (75g) pearl barley*
*3 pints (1.8l) water*
*3 lemons*
*3oz (75g) sugar*

1. Put the barley and water into a pan, bring to the boil and then cover and simmer for 30 minutes. Strain the liquid into a large jug.
2. Peel the lemons very thinly without any white pith. Remove the pith from the lemons and slice the fruit. Put the fruit and lemon peel into the jug with the barley liquid.
3. Stir in the sugar. Leave until cold.
4. Strain into a clean jug. Store in the refrigerator for up to 5 days.

## Fruit Brose

An old-fashioned drink which is refreshing but also nourishing, and is particularly good for children. Adults may prefer it hot with a tot of whisky.

*2oz (50g) medium oatmeal*
*½oz (15g) light soft brown sugar*
*1 lemon or orange*
*½ pint (300ml) boiling water*

1. Mix the oatmeal and sugar in a jug. Add the grated rind and juice of the fruit.
2. Pour on the boiling water and leave covered until cold.
3. Strain, pressing out all the liquid.
4. Dilute to taste with water and serve cold.

## Oatmeal Refresher

Refreshing and sustaining, this is an old-fashioned version of today's soft drinks.

*1 tbsp fine oatmeal*
*1 pint (600ml) water*
*1 tbsp lemon juice*
*sugar to taste*

1. Mix the oatmeal with a little of the water to make a thin paste.
2. Boil the remaining water and pour on to the oatmeal. Stir well and leave to stand for 30 minutes. Strain and stir in the lemon juice.
3. Sweeten to taste and serve cold.

# BEANS AND PULSES

Known collectively as legumes or pulses, these are seeds from pods which we know more familiarly as beans, peas and lentils. A wide variety of pulses is available, and all are cheap and filling. Pulses can be made into complete dishes, or may be served as accompaniments to other foods.

## Buying and Storing

Pulses may be bought from grocers and health food shops, and it is best to buy them from a shop where there is a good regular turnover. Old beans, peas and lentils are not dangerous, but they do take a long time to cook. With today's increasing interest in a healthy diet, shops tend to have much fresher supplies, and there is no need to buy pulses which are thin, dull and wrinkled. Pulses look attractive in glass jars, but if these are in strong sunshine, they will lose their flavour and vital nutrients. The best storage is in airtight containers which are dry and dark, and stone jars are ideal.

## Soaking and Cooking

Many pulses are now beautifully clean and well-presented in boxes or see-through bags. If they have been bought loose however, it is advisable to look through them for pieces of grit, and to rinse them before use.

Lentils and split peas need not be soaked, but all other beans should be soaked for 8-12 hours in plenty of cold water. They will swell up to about three times their size after this soaking. If time is short, pulses may be brought to the boil without soaking, boiled for 5 minutes, then left to stand in the water for 1 hour before final cooking.

After soaking, the pulses should be drained well, rinsed and drained again, and they should not be cooked in the soaking water. Fresh water is needed for cooking, but no salt must be added, as this toughens the skins and increases cooking time. Vinegar and other acidic substances such as tomatoes, have the same effect, and should be added after initial cooking.

When cooking beans, they should be brought to the boil and boiled uncovered for 10 minutes which destroys any toxic elements. The temperature should then be lowered and the beans simmered for the required cooking time. Soya beans need a very long cooking time, and they should be boiled hard for the first hour before cooking is finished by simmering.

Cooking times are given below, but careful judgement is needed according to the dish which is to be made. For a salad, for instance, whole pulses may be needed, while for a soup or pâté a softer texture is desirable. Leftover cooked pulses may be kept in a covered container in the refrigerator for up to 5 days in the refrigerator, but pulses should not be left in the liquid or they will ferment.

## Alternative Cooking Methods

Pulses may be prepared in a *pressure cooker*, which speeds up cooking time considerably. It is important to follow manufacturer's instructions carefully for quantities and timing, as the pulses can collapse quickly into a purée if overcooked. A *slow-cooker* may be used, but red kidney beans must be boiled hard for 10 minutes before putting into the cooker, to eliminate dangerous toxins. There is little advantage in using a *microwave oven* as the pulses will take just as long to cook as by normal methods. Some recipes involve *oven-cooking* which can give a delicious glazed crusty top to dishes which are best cooked in earthenware pots, but when the pulses are pre-boiled they should not be overcooked or they will become mushy.

| Pulses (Soaked) | Average Cooking Time |
|---|---|
| Mung (Chinese) beans | 30-45 minutes |
| Aduki beans, black-eyed beans, canellini, flageolets, red kidney beans | 45-50 minutes |
| Black beans, borlotti, ful medames, haricot beans | 1 hour |
| Butter beans, lima beans, pinto beans, chick peas, whole green peas | 1-1½ hours |
| Soya beans | 2-2½ hours |

| Pulses (Unsoaked) | |
|---|---|
| Split lentils | 15-30 minutes |
| Whole lentils | 30-45 minutes |
| Split peas | 40-45 minutes |

# GLOSSARY OF PULSES

## Aduki Beans (Adzuki)

Grown in China and Korea, and known by the Japanese as 'the king of beans'. Small, hard, round red beans with a nutty flavour.

## Black-eyed Beans
## (Black-eyed Peas, Cow Peas)

Native to Africa, but also grown in America and China. White bean with distinguishing black 'eye' has a savoury flavour and soft fleshy texture when cooked.

## Black Beans

Very popular in Latin America, these are similar in size and texture to red kidney beans (for which they may be substituted) but have shiny black skins.

## Borlotti Beans

Particularly popular in Italy, but also grown in East Africa and Taiwan. Brownish-pink mottled skin with a distinct kidney shape. A full-flavoured bean, the palest one being the sweetest.

## Broad Beans

When dried, these become pale brown and need long cooking, but are rarely used now that more attractive kidney beans are easily available.

## Butter Beans
## (see also Lima Beans)

Grown in tropical areas, these large flat white beans have a creamy flavour and soft texture.

## Canellini Beans (Canneloni)

A pinky-beige bean grown in Argentina and Italy, where it is much used. Canellini beans may be substituted for kidney beans in recipes.

## Flageolet Beans

Attractive haricot beans harvested when young and tender and then dried, resulting in a pale green colour and delicate texture. They are sweet and delicious and much used in Italy and France, particularly in lamb dishes.

### Ful Medames
### (Egyptian Brown Beans)

Small brown beans with smooth skins which are particularly popular in Egypt.

### Haricot Beans
### (White Haricots, Navy Beans, Great Northern Beans)

Small, oval greyish-white beans used for 'baked beans'. Originating in Central and South America, they are widely grown in the United States. In France, stews which contain them are also known as 'haricots'.

### Lima Beans

Originating from Peru, these are like small butter beans, with a sweeter flavour.

### Mung (Chinese) Beans

Very small green beans originating in tropical Asia, these may be cooked as pulses, but are widely used to produce beansprouts, which are particularly popular for Chinese dishes.

### Pinto Beans

Similar to borlotti, these haricot beans are heavily speckled, but turn pink when cooked.

### Red Kidney Beans
### (Chilli Beans)

Richly-coloured kidney beans which are particularly popular in Mexican dishes. They must be boiled hard at the beginning of cooking to destroy any toxic elements.

### Soya Beans

Originating in China, these beans are the most nutritious of all, being the only legume which provides complete protein. They take a very long time to cook and are bland in flavour, and are often used as a meat substitute.

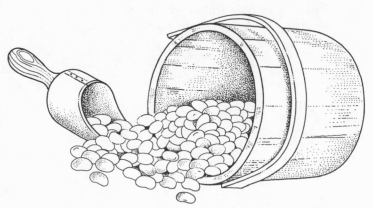

## Chick Peas
### (Garbanzos, Garbanzo Peas)

Hard round peas which look like dried hazelnuts, are high in protein and are sometimes ground into flour. The older they are, the earthier the flavour. Used widely in Mediterranean, Middle Eastern and Indian cookery.

## Whole Peas
### (Marrow Fat Peas)

Dull green wrinkled peas which have a floury texture when cooked, and which are most often used for soups and purées.

## Split Peas

The inner part of the pea which is split in half, and which is available in green and yellow varieties. Split peas cook quickly and become very soft, so are mostly used for soups.

## Lentils

Originating from the eastern Mediterranean, but now grown in the Middle East and India, and available whole and split. Red lentils are bright orange but become yellow when cooked and have a savoury flavour. Green lentils (sometimes known as Egyptian lentils) are dull green in colour with a fresh spicy flavour. Brown lentils (sometimes known as Chinese lentils) are dark dull brown with a rich flavour.

Many beans, peas and lentils are sold ready-cooked in cans, and are useful for preparing dishes when time is short for both soaking and cooking. Canned pulses tend to be rather soft and allowance should be made for this when adding them to recipes so that they do not become overcooked and disintegrate.

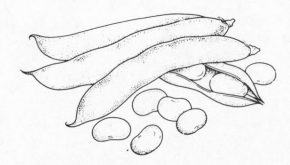

# BEANS AND PULSES

## Three Bean Soup

A colourful soup which is full of flavour and which makes a nourishing complete meal.

*4oz (100g) haricot beans*
*2oz (50g) red kidney beans*
*2oz (50g) flageolet beans*
*2 medium onions*
*2 medium carrots*
*2 celery sticks*
*2 garlic cloves*
*1oz (25g) butter*
*14oz (400g) can tomatoes*
*½ pint (300ml) stock*
*¼ pint (150ml) red wine*
*1 tbsp tomato purée*
*1 tbsp Worcestershire sauce*
*1 bay leaf*
*sprig of thyme*
*sprig of parsley*
*salt and pepper*
*1oz (25g) grated Parmesan cheese*

1. Soak each type of bean separately in cold water overnight. Drain well and rinse in cold water. Drain and put the beans in a large pan. Cover with cold water, bring to the boil and boil for 10 minutes. Cover and simmer for 1 hour until the beans are tender but unbroken. Drain well.
2. Chop the onions, carrots and celery finely. Crush the garlic. Melt the butter and cook the vegetables until soft and golden.
3. Add the tomatoes and their juice, stock, wine, tomato purée, Worcestershire sauce, herbs, salt and pepper. Bring to the boil, cover and simmer for 20 minutes. Remove the herbs.
4. Add the beans and simmer for 10 minutes.
5. Serve hot sprinkled with Parmesan cheese.

## Pea Soup With Tarragon

A delicious soup made from dried peas flavoured with fresh tarragon. In the winter, dried tarragon may be used, but the quantity should be halved.

*8oz (225g) dried peas*
*2 pints (1.2l) water*
*2 tbsps fresh tarragon*
*2 tbsps single cream*
*salt and pepper*

1. Soak the peas in cold water overnight.
2. Drain well and cover with water. Bring to the boil, boil for 10 minutes and then simmer for 1-1¼ hours until soft.
3. Add the tarragon and continue simmering for 5 minutes.
4. Rub through a sieve or blend in a liquidizer.
5. Reheat, stir in the cream and season to taste.

## Summer Bean and Basil Soup

A simple vegetable soup which is enhanced by the basil sauce, and which makes a complete meal if served with crusty white or wholemeal bread.

*1lb (450g) haricot beans*
*3 medium carrots*
*3 leeks*
*3 medium potatoes*
*3 courgettes*
*8oz (225g) French beans*
*4oz (100g) short macaroni*
*salt and pepper*
*4 garlic cloves*
*1oz (25g) fresh basil leaves*
*2oz (50g) grated Parmesan cheese*
*¼ pint (150ml) olive oil*

1. Soak the beans in cold water overnight. Drain well. Cover in fresh cold water and bring to the boil. Cover and simmer for 1 hour, and drain well.

2. Slice the carrots and leeks thinly, and dice the potatoes. Put into a large pan with the haricot beans. Cover with 5 pints (3 litres) water. Bring to the boil and then simmer without a lid for 30 minutes.

3. Slice the courgettes thickly without peeling. Cut the French beans into small chunks. Add to the soup with the macaroni and plenty of salt and pepper. Bring to the boil again and simmer for 20 minutes.

4. While the soup is cooking, prepare the basil sauce by crushing the garlic and basil leaves to a smooth paste (this may be done in a liquidizer or food processor). Stir in the cheese and plenty of seasoning, and gradually stir in the oil. Serve separately with the hot soup.

## Chick Pea and Pasta Soup

This soup takes quite a long time to cook, but it is very good and tasty and well worth the effort.

*1lb (450g) chick peas*
*5 tbsps olive oil*
*2 garlic cloves*
*4 anchovy fillets*
*4 tomatoes*
*3 tbsps chopped fresh parsley*
*2 tsps fresh rosemary*
*2 pints (1.2l) water*
*8oz (225g) short macaroni*
*salt and pepper*
*Parmesan cheese*

1. Soak the chick peas overnight in cold water. Drain well. Cover with fresh cold water, bring to the boil, then simmer for 1½ hours. Drain well and reserve.

2. Heat the oil and stir in the crushed garlic and very finely chopped anchovies. Cook very gently for 5 minutes over low heat, stirring well.

3. Skin the tomatoes, remove seeds and chop the flesh roughly. Add to the pan with the parsley, rosemary and water. Add the drained chick peas. Bring to the boil, cover and simmer for 30 minutes, stirring often.

4. Cook the macaroni in plenty of boiling salted water for 8 minutes. Drain well and add to the soup.

5. Simmer for 15 minutes and serve with plenty of Parmesan cheese.

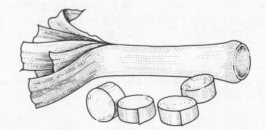

## Black Bean Soup

A thick creamy soup which may be made with red kidney beans. A garnish of soured cream makes a pleasing contrast.

*1lb (450g) black beans*
*2 pints (1.2l) stock or water*
*1 bay leaf*
*salt and pepper*
*1 large onion*
*1 garlic clove*
*3 tbsps oil*
*2 tbsps red wine*
*½ pint (300ml) milk*
*¼ pint (150ml) soured cream*

1. Soak the beans in cold water overnight. Drain well and put into a pan with the stock or water and bay leaf. Bring to the boil, cover and simmer for 1¼ hours.

2. Put through a sieve or blend in a liquidizer, discarding the bay leaf. Season well with salt and pepper and return to a clean pan.

3. Chop the onion finely and crush the garlic. Cook in the oil over low heat until soft and golden. Add to the bean purée with the wine. Add enough milk to give the required thickness.

4. Reheat gently and add more salt and pepper if liked.

5. Serve with a spoonful of soured cream in each bowl.

## Roman Bean Soup

A colourful mixture of vegetables and beans which may be varied according to the flavour of the stock used. A little crumbed crisp bacon makes a tasty garnish.

*8oz (225g) haricot or butter beans*
*2 pints (1.2l) stock*
*1 large onion*
*1 large carrot*
*1 celery stick*
*4 tomatoes*
*1 garlic clove*
*½ lemon*
*1 bay leaf*
*salt and pepper*
*2 tbsps chopped fresh parsley*

1. Soak the beans in cold water overnight.

2. Drain well and cover with stock.

3. Add chopped onion, carrot, celery. Skin the tomatoes and remove the seeds. Chop the flesh roughly and add to the pan. Add crushed garlic, grated rind and juice of the lemon and the bay leaf.

4. Bring to the boil, cover and simmer for 1½ hours, adding more water or stock if necessary.

5. Discard the bay leaf. Put half the soup into a liquidizer and blend until smooth.

6. Return to the soup and season to taste. Bring to the boil and serve hot sprinkled with parsley.

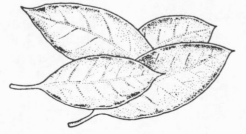

# Lentil Soup

A pleasantly textured soup which is very filling. If liked, bacon stock may be used instead of water.

*8oz (225g) lentils*
*1 large onion*
*1 bay leaf*
*2 garlic cloves*
*½ tsp ground cumin*
*2 pints (1.2l) water*
*1 tbsp chopped fresh parsley*
*½oz (15g) butter*
*1 tbsp oil*

1. Put the lentils into a pan. Chop the onion finely and put half the pieces in the pan. Add the bay leaf, 1 crushed garlic clove, cumin and water. Cover and simmer for 40 minutes.
2. Melt the butter and oil and cook the remaining onion and crushed garlic until soft and golden.
3. Put the fried onion into a liquidizer with half the lentils and blend until smooth, or put through a sieve.
4. Return to the pan and bring back to the boil. Garnish with parsley.

# Swedish Pea Soup

This is the traditional Thursday meal in Sweden, followed by pancakes with jam.

*8oz (225g) split peas*
*8oz (225g) salt pork belly*
*1 medium onion*
*1½ pints (900ml) water*
*salt and pepper*

1. Put the peas and pork into a pan. Add the chopped onion and water.
2. Bring to the boil, cover and simmer for 1½ hours until the peas are very soft.
3. Lift out the pork and cut into slices. Put on to a serving plate.
4. Season the soup with salt and pepper to taste. Serve hot with the pork on a side-dish to be eaten separately with mustard.

# Italian Bean Soup

A soothing creamy soup which makes a complete meal with wholemeal bread.

*8oz (225g) haricot beans*
*pinch of ground ginger*
*2 pints (1.2l) milk*
*1 small onion*
*salt and pepper*
*2 egg yolks*
*1oz (25g) melted butter*
*1 tbsp chopped fresh parsley*
*fried bread cubes (optional)*

1. Soak the beans overnight in cold water. Drain well and then put into a pan of fresh cold water. Bring to the boil, boil for 10 minutes and simmer for 45 minutes. Drain well.
2. Put into a pan with the ginger, milk, finely chopped onion, salt and pepper. Bring to the boil and then simmer for 2 hours, stirring often.
3. Beat the egg yolks and butter together in a bowl and add a few spoonfuls of the hot soup. Beat well and add to the soup.
4. Reheat gently and serve garnished with parsley. If liked, serve with fried bread cubes.

## Soya Pâté

A useful spread for toast or biscuits, with the smooth paste offset by crunchy sesame seeds.

*8oz (225g) soya beans*
*1 medium onion*
*1oz (25g) butter*
*2 tbsps tomato purée*
*2 tbsps chopped black olives*
*1 tbsp chopped fresh parsley*
*pinch of salt*
*1 tbsp sesame seeds*

1. Soak the beans overnight in cold water.
2. Drain the beans well, cover in fresh water and bring to the boil. Boil for 10 minutes, cover and simmer for about 2½ hours until the beans are very soft. Drain well.
3. Chop the onion finely and cook in the butter until soft and golden.
4. Mash the beans well and stir in the onion and butter, tomato purée, olives, parsley and salt.
5. Put the sesame seeds into a small pan and toss over low heat until lightly browned. Stir into the bean mixture.
6. Spoon into a serving dish and chill for 30 minutes before serving.

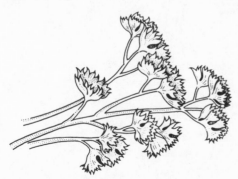

## Hummous

A creamy pâté which is full of flavour. It may be served as part of a salad meal, or as a spread for crusty bread.

*4oz (100g) chick peas*
*2 garlic cloves*
*2 tbsps tahini*
*2 tbsps olive oil*
*1 tbsp lemon juice*
*salt and pepper*
*2 tsps chopped fresh mint*

1. Soak the chick peas in cold water overnight.
2. Drain them well and cover with fresh cold water. Bring to the boil and then simmer for about 2 hours until soft. Drain and reserve 8 tablespoons cooking liquid.
3. Put the cooked chick peas into a liquidizer with the peeled garlic, tahini, oil, lemon juice, salt and pepper. Add the reserved liquid. Blend to a soft creamy paste. Adjust seasoning.
4. Spoon into a serving bowl and sprinkle with mint.

## Southern Beanpot

Although this is a simple version of the traditional *cassoulet*, it still takes a little time to make and quite a lot of ingredients, so is worth making in this large quantity which will serve 8 people.

*1½lb (675g) haricot beans*
*1 large onion*
*4 garlic cloves*
*1lb (450g) piece smoked bacon*
*1 bay leaf*
*sprig of thyme*
*sprig of parsley*
*2 duck portions*
*1lb (450g) pork belly*
*8oz (225g) garlic sausage*
*1lb (450g) tomatoes*
*salt and pepper*
*2oz (50g) fresh breadcrumbs*

1. Soak the beans in cold water overnight.
2. Drain well and cover with fresh cold water. Bring to the boil and add the chopped onion and garlic, the piece of bacon, bay leaf, thyme and parsley. Cover and simmer for 1½ hours.
3. While the beans are cooking, put the duck portions and piece of pork on a rack in a roasting tin. Roast at 200°C (400°C), gas mark 6 for 1 hour.
4. Drain the beans and reserve the liquid. Take out the bacon and cut into chunks.
5. Cut the duck portions, pork and garlic sausage into chunks.
6. Skin the tomatoes, discard pips, and chop the flesh roughly.
7. Using a deep earthenware casserole, arrange layers of meat, beans and tomatoes, seasoning each layer well with salt and pepper. Pour in some of the reserved liquid to come halfway up the layers.
8. Cover and cook at 160°C (325°F), gas mark 3 for 1½ hours.
9. Remove the lid. Add a little more liquid if necessary to come up to the halfway mark. Sprinkle on breadcrumbs in a layer.
10. Continue baking for 1½ hours. Serve with crusty bread and a salad.

# Cheese and Lentil Loaf

A tasty loaf which is nicest served hot with tomato or mushroom sauce and a salad or vegetables.

*12oz (350g) lentils*
*1 large onion*
*1oz (25g) butter*
*8oz (225g) grated Cheddar cheese*
*3oz (75g) brown breadcrumbs*
*1 egg*
*2 tbsps single cream*
*1 tbsp tomato ketchup*
*1 tbsp chopped fresh parsley*
*pinch of ground nutmeg*
*salt and pepper*

1. Cover the lentils with cold water and bring to the boil. Cover and simmer for about 40 minutes until tender. Drain well and put into a bowl.

2. Chop the onion finely and cook in the butter until soft and golden.

3. Add the onion to the lentils with the cheese, breadcrumbs, beaten egg, cream, ketchup and parsley. Season to taste with nutmeg, salt and pepper.

4. Grease a 1½lb (675g) loaf tin and put in the lentil mixture.

5. Bake at 180°C (350°F), gas mark 4 for 45 minutes. Leave in the tin for 5 minutes, and turn on to a warm serving dish.

# Summer Lentil Stew

Vegetables add flavour and form a rich sauce for the lentils in this stew which may be a main dish or an accompaniment to meat, poultry or fish.

*2 tbsps oil*
*2 medium onions*
*2 celery sticks*
*4 small courgettes*
*4 tomatoes*
*1 garlic clove*
*1½ pints (900ml) stock or water*
*¼ tsp ground coriander*
*salt and pepper*
*8oz (225g) lentils*
*2 tbsps chopped fresh parsley*

1. Heat the oil in a large pan. Add chopped onions and sliced celery.

2. Do not peel the courgettes, but slice them thinly and add to the pan. Skin the tomatoes and remove the seeds. Chop the flesh roughly and add to the pan.

3. Add the crushed garlic. Fry gently until the vegetables are soft and golden, stirring well.

4. Add the stock or water, coriander, salt and pepper. Bring to the boil and add the lentils. Cover and simmer for 1 hour until the lentils are tender and most of the liquid has been absorbed.

5. Serve hot, sprinkled with parsley.

## Butter Bean Pie

For speed, a can of butter beans may be used for this pie, which is good served with a crisp green salad.

*1lb (450g) butter beans*
*1 large onion*
*1oz (25g) butter*
*4oz (100g) button mushrooms*
*1lb (450g) canned tomatoes*
*1 tbsp tomato purée*
*½ tsp basil*
*salt and pepper*

Pastry
*6oz (150g) wholemeal flour*
*pinch of salt*
*3oz (75g) hard margarine or butter*
*4 tbsps cold water*

1. Soak the butter beans overnight in cold water. Drain well and cover with fresh cold water. Bring to the boil, cover and simmer for about 1¼ hours until tender. Drain well.
2. Chop the onion finely and cook in butter until soft and golden. Lift out the onion and reserve. Quarter the mushrooms and cook in the butter for 3 minutes, stirring well.
3. Mix together the beans, onions, mushrooms, tomatoes and their juice, tomato purée, basil and plenty of seasoning. Put into an 8in (20cm) pie dish and leave until cold.
4. To make the pastry, rub the fat into the flour and salt and mix with the water. Roll out and cover the bean mixture and cut a slit in the centre.
5. Bake at 200°C (400°F), gas mark 6 for 30 minutes.

## Soya Roast

A bean loaf which may be served hot with vegetables, and perhaps with a tomato or mushroom sauce.

*8oz (225g) soya beans*
*1 small onion*
*4oz (100g) toasted breadcrumbs*
*¼ pint (150ml) milk*
*1 tbsp oil*
*1 tsp soy sauce*
*½ tsp dried thyme*
*¼ tsp celery salt*
*salt and pepper*

1. Soak the beans overnight in cold water. Drain well and rinse in cold water. Cover with fresh cold water, bring to the boil and boil for 10 minutes. Lower heat, cover and simmer for 2½ hours until beans are soft. Drain well.
2. Mash the beans in a bowl. Chop the onion finely and add to the beans with the other ingredients, seasoning with salt and pepper to taste.
3. Oil a 1lb (450g) loaf tin and pack in the bean mixture. Bake at 180°C (350°F), gas mark 4 for 40 minutes.
4. Turn out and serve in slices.

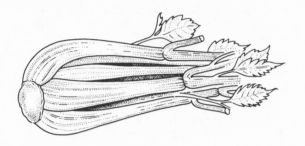

## Hoppin' John

A simple mixture of beans and rice which makes a light meal or may be an accompaniment to meat, poultry or fish.

*4oz (100g) black-eye beans*
*1 pint (600ml) stock*
*1lb (450g) tomatoes*
*4oz (100g) long-grain rice*
*salt and pepper*
*pinch of cayenne pepper*
*2 tbsps chopped fresh parsley*

1. Soak the beans in cold water overnight. Drain well and put into a pan with the stock. Bring to the boil, cover and simmer for 1 hour.
2. Skin the tomatoes and deseed them. Chop the flesh roughly. Add to the pan with the rice. Bring to the boil again, then simmer for 15 minutes.
3. Season well with salt and pepper, and add a little cayenne pepper and half the parsley. Stir well and leave to stand for 5 minutes.
4. Put into a warm serving dish and sprinkle with remaining parsley.

## Soya Bean Loaf

A tasty baked loaf which may be served hot or cold with a vegetable sauce and a salad.

*8oz (225g) soya beans*
*1 chicken stock cube*
*1 slice onion*
*¼ pint (150ml) tomato juice*
*1 tsp Worcestershire sauce*
*pinch of sage*
*salt and pepper*
*1 green pepper*
*1 celery stick*
*1 medium carrot*

1. Soak the beans over night in cold water. Drain well. Cover with fresh cold water, bring to the boil and simmer for 2 hours until the beans are soft. Drain well.
2. Put the beans into a liquidizer or food processor with the stock cube, onion, tomato juice, sauce, sage, salt and pepper. Blend until smooth.
3. Chop the pepper and celery finely. Grate the carrot coarsely. Mix into the bean purée.
4. Place in a greased 1lb (450g) loaf tin. Bake at 200°C (400°F), gas mark 6 for 45 minutes. Turn on to a warm serving dish.

## Chick Pea Flan with Oat Pastry

The smooth and tasty filling is a pleasant contrast to a textured pastry and is offset by fresh tasting tomatoes and olives.

*12oz (350g) chick peas*
*1 large onion*
*stock or water*
*2 garlic cloves*
*1 tbsp tahini*
*1 tbsp lemon juice*
*3 tbsps oil*
*6 tomatoes*
*10 stoned black olives*
*2 tbsps chopped fresh parsley*
*salt*

Pastry
*6oz (150g) plain flour*
*2oz (50g) rolled oats*
*pinch of salt*
*1 tsp dried mixed herbs*
*4oz (100g) vegetable margarine*
*3 tbsps water*

1. Wash the chick peas well under running water. Cover with cold water and soak overnight. Drain well, rinse, and put into a saucepan with stock or water to cover.

2. Slice the onion and add to the pan. Bring to the boil, boil for 10 minutes, then cover and simmer for about 1½ hours until peas are soft, and liquid has almost evaporated.

3. Put into liquidizer with garlic, tahini, lemon juice and oil, and blend until smooth (or put through a sieve).

4. Peel half the tomatoes, and cut into quarters. Discard the seeds and chop the flesh roughly. Fold into the chick pea mixture and season with salt to taste. Chill while making the pastry.

5. Mix together flour, oats, salt and herbs. Rub in the margarine and make into a dough with water. Roll out and line a 9in (22.5cm) flan tin. Prick lightly and cover with a piece of greaseproof paper. Fill the flan case with baking beans. Bake at 200°C (400°F), gas mark 6 for 35 minutes.

6. Cool slightly, remove carefully from tin and allow to become cold. Spread in the chick pea mixture.

7. Slice the remaining tomatoes and arrange on top of the flan. Garnish with olives and sprinkle with parsley. Serve with salad.

## Lentil and Vegetable Stew

A thick rich mixture of lentils and vegetables which makes a complete meal served with wholemeal bread.

*2 medium onions*
*1 garlic clove*
*2 celery sticks*
*4 courgettes*
*4 tomatoes*
*2 tbsps oil*
*1½ pints (900ml) water or stock*
*8oz (225g) lentils*
*pinch of ground coriander*
*salt and pepper*
*1 tbsp chopped fresh parsley*

1. Peel the onions and chop them finely. Crush the garlic. Slice the celery and the courgettes without peeling.
2. Heat the oil and cook the vegetables over low heat for 10 minutes until soft and golden, stirring frequently.
3. Peel the tomatoes and discard the seeds. Chop the flesh roughly and add to the pan with the water or stock, lentils, coriander, salt and pepper.
4. Bring to the boil, cover and simmer for 1½ hours. Serve hot sprinkled with parsley.

## Bean and Vegetable Casserole

A flavour-packed meal which may be prepared with cans of beans and pulses.

*1 large onion*
*1oz (25g) butter*
*1 garlic clove*
*4oz (100g) French beans*
*3 courgettes*
*4oz (100g) button mushrooms*
*7floz (200ml) chicken stock*
*salt and pepper*
*2 bay leaves*
*sprig of thyme or rosemary*
*2 × 1lb (450g) cans Barbecue Beans*
*11½oz (335g) can sweetcorn kernels*
*4 tbsps canned chick peas*
*8 small slices French bread*
*1oz (25g) butter*
*1½oz (40g) grated Cheddar cheese*

1. Slice the onion thinly and fry gently in the butter for 5 minutes. Add crushed garlic and continue frying for 1 minute. Put into a casserole.
2. Add topped and tailed beans, thickly sliced courgettes, mushrooms, stock, seasoning and herbs.
3. Cover and cook at 180°C (350°F) gas mark 4 for 25 minutes.
4. Stir in the Barbecue Beans, drained sweetcorn and chick peas. Cover and continue baking for 20 minutes.
5. Spread the bread with butter and sprinkle with cheese. Put under a hot grill until bubbling and golden.
6. Serve the casserole very hot, topped with the cheese slices.

## Mexican Beans

This version of *chilli con carne* is spicy with a creamy texture. It is very good served with wholemeal bread and a green salad.

*8oz (225g) red kidney beans*
*1 large onion*
*1 garlic clove*
*1 tbsp oil*
*1lb (450g) raw minced beef*
*2 tsps chilli powder*
*½ tsp sugar*
*pinch of ground cumin*
*1lb (450g) canned tomatoes*
*1oz (25g) tomato purée*

1. Soak the beans overnight in cold water. Drain well and cover with fresh cold water. Bring to the boil, cover and simmer for 1 hour. Drain well. If preferred, canned beans may be used, which only need draining.

2. Chop the onion finely and crush the garlic clove. Cook in the oil until soft and golden.

3. Add the meat and stir over low heat until the meat is well browned. Stir well so that the pieces of meat remain separate. Add the chilli powder and cook for 1 minute.

4. Stir in the sugar, cumin, tomatoes and their juice and tomato purée. Simmer for 30 minutes, stirring occasionally.

5. Add the beans and simmer for 15 minutes, stirring occasionally. Serve hot.

## Baked Lentils with Sausages

A slow-cooking, comforting dish for a winter night which is best made with really good all-meat pork sausages and brown lentils.

*1lb (450g) pork sausages*
*1 large onion*
*8oz (225g) lentils*
*1 garlic clove*
*2 cloves*
*1 bay leaf*
*salt and pepper*

1. Grill the sausages lightly until the skins are golden brown. Arrange in an ovenware casserole.
2. Chop the onion finely. Sprinkle the onion, lentils and crushed garlic over the sausages.
3. Add the cloves and bay leaf and season well with salt and pepper.
4. Cover with water or stock. Cover and bake at 150°C (300°F), gas mark 2 for 2½ hours until the lentils are very soft and the liquid has been absorbed. Discard the cloves and bay leaf, and adjust the seasoning before serving.

## Haricot Beef

A slow-cooking dish which is rich and succulent. The beans do not need pre-cooking as they will simmer for a long time with the beef.

*4oz (100g) haricot beans*
*1 large onion*
*2 tbsps oil*
*1lb (450g) shin beef*
*1 pint (600ml) water*
*½ pint (300ml) tomato juice*
*3 tbsps tomato purée*
*pinch of mustard powder*
*salt and pepper*

1. Soak the beans overnight in cold water. Drain well.
2. Chop the onion finely and cook in the oil over low heat until soft and golden.
3. Cut the beef into cubes and add to the pan, cooking until the meat is sealed on all sides.
4. Transfer the meat and onions to a casserole with the beans. Mix the water, juice, tomato purée and mustard powder and pour over the meat.
5. Cover and cook at 150°C (300°F), gas mark 2 for 3 hours.

## Spring Lamb Casserole

Red kidney beans or flageolets are usually part of this dish, but black beans or haricot beans may be used instead. The canned variety will speed up the preparation of the recipe.

*4oz (100g) dried beans*
*1½lb (675g) shoulder lamb*
*2 leeks*
*3 tbsps oil*
*2 tbsps lemon juice*
*2 tsps turmeric*
*1 tsp fresh dill*
*1 tsp chopped fresh mint*
*salt and pepper*

1. Soak the beans overnight in cold water. Drain well and cover in fresh cold water. Bring to the boil, cover and simmer for 1 hour. Drain well and reserve.
2. Cut the lamb in cubes and fry in the oil until golden-brown on all sides. Drain the lamb and put into a casserole.
3. Slice the leeks thinly and cook in the oil until soft and golden. Drain and add to the lamb.
4. Add lemon juice, turmeric, dill, mint, salt and pepper. Cover with 1 pint (600ml) water.
5. Cover and cook on low heat on top of the stove (or at 160°C (325°F), gas mark 3) for 1 hour. Stir in the beans and continue cooking for 20 minutes.
6. Serve hot with seasonal vegetables or salad.

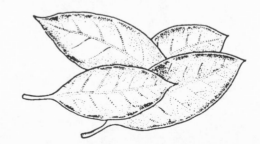

## Southern Baked Beans

Beans with a rich tomato-flavoured sauce which make a good meal if served with plenty of wholemeal bread, or which may be an accompaniment to other dishes.

*8oz (225g) haricot beans*
*1 pint (600ml) water*
*1 large onion*
*2 celery sticks*
*1 red pepper*
*4 tomatoes*
*1 tbsp black treacle*
*1 tbsp tomato purée*
*1 tbsp vinegar*
*2 tbsps Worcestershire sauce*
*2 tsps mustard powder*
*salt and pepper*

1. Soak the beans in cold water overnight.
2. Drain well and cover with cold water. Bring to the boil, cover and simmer for 1 hour. Drain and reserve ½ pint (300ml) cooking liquid.
3. Chop the onion and slice the celery and pepper. Skin the tomatoes and chop the flesh roughly. Mix the vegetables together.
4. Arrange the beans in alternating layers with the vegetables in a casserole. Mix the reserved liquid with black treacle, tomato purée, vinegar, Worcestershire sauce, mustard, salt and pepper. Pour into the casserole.
5. Cover and bake at 180°C (350°F), gas mark 4 for 1½ hours. Serve hot.

## French Lamb with Flageolets

Lamb is often combined with dried beans in France, and the pretty green flageolets make particularly attractive dishes. Haricot beans may be used if preferred.

*1lb (450g) flageolet beans*
*3-4lb (1.5-2kg) boned leg of lamb*
*3 garlic cloves*
*salt and pepper*
*8oz (225g) fat bacon*
*2 tbsps oil*
*2 medium onions*
*3 cloves*
*1 medium carrot*
*1lb (450g) potatoes*

1. Soak the beans overnight in cold water. Drain well.
2. Tie the lamb firmly into a roll. Make tiny slits with a sharp knife all over the surface and insert tiny pieces of garlic. Season well with salt and pepper.
3. Cut the bacon into small strips. Heat the oil and brown the lamb on all sides. Add the bacon and cook for 5 minutes. Cover and cook at 180°C (350°F), gas mark 4 for 1 hour.
4. While the lamb is cooking, put the beans into a pan and cover with water. Add 1 onion stuck with cloves and the carrot. Bring to the boil, cover and simmer for 1 hour. Drain the beans, reserving the liquid and discarding the onion and carrot.
5. Lift the lamb from the roasting tin. Slice the remaining onion and mix with sliced potatoes and drained beans. Put the vegetables into the tin and put the lamb on top. Add 1½ pints (900ml) strained cooking liquid. Cover and continue cooking for 45 minutes.

## Autumn Chick Pea Casserole

A comforting dish which is suitable for eating hot or cold. It goes well with a salad and wholemeal bread.

2oz (50g) chick peas
1 large onion
2 garlic cloves
4 tbsps oil
3 potatoes
2 tomatoes
1 tbsp tomato purée
½ tsp mixed fresh herbs
salt and pepper
1 pint (300ml) stock or water

1. Soak the chick peas overnight in cold water. Drain well.
2. Chop the onion finely and crush the garlic. Heat the oil and cook the onion and garlic until soft and golden.
3. Add the chick peas and thinly sliced potatoes. Fry until the potatoes are golden.
4. Skin the tomatoes and deseed them. Chop the flesh roughly and add to the pan with tomato purée, herbs, salt and pepper.
5. Add the stock or water. Bring slowly to the boil, cover and simmer for 1 hour until the potatoes and chick peas are soft.

## Lentil and Tomato Bake

A good side dish to serve with curry, but particularly delicious if pork sausages are placed on the mixture during baking.

8oz (225g) lentils
1 pint (600ml) water
1 medium onion
1 tbsp oil
1lb (450g) canned tomatoes
1 green pepper
salt and pepper

1. Put the lentils and water into a pan with a pinch of salt. Bring to the boil and simmer for about 45 minutes until the lentils are soft.
2. Chop the onion finely and cook in the oil until soft and golden. Stir into the lentils.
3. Drain the tomatoes (saving the liquid for soup). Chop the tomatoes roughly and mix with the lentils. Add finely chopped green pepper and season well.
4. Put the mixture into a greased ovenware dish and bake at 150°C (300°F), gas mark 2 for 1 hour. Serve hot.

## Pepper Beanpot

A richly-flavoured mixture of beans, tomatoes and pepper which is very good with wholemeal bread and a salad.

*12oz (350g) haricot beans*
*2 tbsps oil*
*1 large onion*
*1 garlic clove*
*1 tbsp paprika*
*2 tbsps tomato purée*
*1 red pepper*
*1lb (450g) canned tomatoes*
*¼ pint (150ml) water*
*salt and pepper*
*4 tbsps soured cream*

1. Soak the beans in cold water overnight.
2. Drain well and cover in fresh cold water. Bring to the boil and simmer for 1 hour. Drain well.
3. Heat the oil in a large pan and fry the chopped onion and crushed garlic until soft and golden. Add the paprika and cook for 2 minutes, stirring well.
4. Add the beans, tomato purée, sliced pepper, tomatoes and their juice, water, salt and pepper. Bring to the boil cover and simmer for 15 minutes.
5. Stir in the soured cream just before serving.

## Haricot Beans with Tomato Herb Sauce

A perfect summer dish of beans which can make a light meal, or accompany fish, meat or poultry. Canned tomatoes may be substituted for fresh ones.

*1lb (450g) haricot beans*
*1 medium onion*
*2 garlic cloves*
*1 tbsp olive oil*
*1lb (450g) tomatoes*
*1 tbsp clear honey*
*salt and pepper*
*2 tbsps chopped fresh parsley*
*1 tbsp fresh thyme*
*2 tsps chopped fresh marjoram*

1. Soak the beans in cold water overnight.
2. Drain the beans well, cover in fresh cold water and bring to the boil. Boil for 10 minutes, cover and simmer for 1 hour. Drain well.
3. Chop the onion finely and crush the garlic. Fry in the oil over low heat until soft and golden.
4. Skin the tomatoes and deseed them. Chop the flesh roughly and add to the onions with the honey, salt and pepper. Simmer for 10 minutes, stirring well.
5. Add the beans and simmer for 5 minutes. Stir in the herbs just before serving.

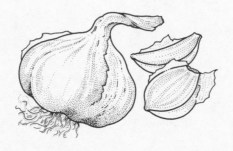

## Farmhouse Beans

Other types of beans may be used for this dish, but butter beans have a slighty floury texture which goes well with the creamy cheese sauce and slightly crisp vegetables.

*8oz (225g) butter beans*
*1 medium onion*
*2 celery sticks*
*1 bay leaf*
*1½oz (40g) butter*
*1½oz (40g) plain flour*
*¾ pint (450ml) milk*
*2oz (50g) grated Cheddar cheese*
*pinch of ground nutmeg*
*salt and pepper*
*2 tomatoes*
*1 tbsp grated Parmesan cheese*
*1 tbsp chopped fresh parsley*

## Honey-baked Beans

A variation on the traditional baked beans which has a subtle flavour. The beans are very good served with fresh tomato sauce.

*8oz (225g) haricot beans*
*3 tomatoes*
*1 medium onion*
*3 lean bacon rashers*
*3oz (75g) clear honey*
*1 tsp French mustard*
*pepper*
*2 tbsps olive oil*

1. Soak the beans overnight in cold water. Drain well. Cover with fresh cold water, bring to the boil and then simmer for 1 hour. Drain well and put into a greased ovenware dish.
2. Skin the tomatoes and discard the seeds. Chop the flesh roughly. Chop the onion and bacon rashers finely.
3. Add the tomatoes, onion, bacon, honey, mustard and a good seasoning of pepper to the beans and stir well. Pour over the olive oil.
4. Cover and bake at 160°C (325°F), gas mark 3 for 2 hours.

1. Soak the beans overnight in cold water. Drain well and cover with fresh cold water.
2. Add chopped onion and celery, and the bay leaf. Bring to the boil and then simmer for 1 hour. Drain well and discard the bay leaf.
3. Melt the butter and work in the flour. Cook for 1 minute and gradually work in the milk. Stir over low heat until the sauce is thick and creamy.
4. Take off the heat and stir in the Cheddar cheese, nutmeg, salt and pepper.
5. Mix the beans, onion and celery with the cheese sauce and place in a greased ovenware dish. Slice the tomatoes and arrange on top, and sprinkle with the Parmesan cheese.
6. Grill under medium heat until golden, and sprinkle with chopped parsley.

# Lentil Rissoles

Crisply-fried lentil cakes which may be served with tomato or mushroom sauce, or with yoghurt flavoured with plenty of garlic and mixed herbs.

8oz (225g) lentils
1 pint (600ml) water
1 tsp ground coriander
salt and pepper
1 medium onion
2 medium carrots
2 celery sticks
2 tbsps oil
6oz (150g) wholemeal breadcrumbs
2 tbsps chopped fresh parsley
1oz (25g) wholemeal plain flour
1 egg
oil for frying

1. Put the lentils into a pan with the water, coriander, salt and pepper.
2. Chop the onion, carrots and celery. Cook in the oil until soft and golden. Add to the lentils and continue cooking for 1 hour until the lentils are soft.
3. Stir in half the breadcrumbs and the parsley. Place on a shallow dish and leave until cold.
4. Shape the mixture into 8 flat cakes. Coat with the flour, then beaten egg and finally the remaining breadcrumbs.
5. Fry in shallow oil until crisp and golden on both sides. Serve hot with a sauce.

# Curried Lentils

Known as *dahl*, this tasty lentil dish is an accompaniment to curry, but it is also good with meat, poultry, sausages, game or fish.

8oz (225g) lentils
1 pint (600ml) stock or water
pinch of salt
1 tsp turmeric
1 tbsp oil
1 medium onion
1 tsp curry powder
1 tsp curry paste
1 tsp garam masala
2 tsps chopped fresh herbs

1. Put the lentils into a pan with the stock or water, salt and turmeric. Bring to the boil and then simmer for about 45 minutes until the lentils are soft and the liquid has been absorbed.
2. Heat the oil and cook the finely chopped onion until soft and golden.
3. Stir in the curry powder, curry paste, garam masala and herbs, and cook over low heat for 3 minutes.
4. Stir in the lentils, reheat and serve hot.

# Roman Lentils

Serve this with plenty of crusty white or wholemeal bread, or serve as an accompaniment to lamb or pork dishes.

1lb (450g) lentils
2 medium onions
2 garlic cloves
¼ pint (150ml) olive oil
1½lb (675g) tomatoes
salt and pepper

1. Cover the lentils with cold water and bring to the boil. Cover and simmer for 30 minutes.
2. Chop the onions finely and crush the garlic. Heat the oil and cook the onions and garlic until soft and golden.
3. Skin and deseed the tomatoes and chop the flesh roughly. Add to the onions and stir over low heat for 5 minutes.
4. Add the lentils and cooking liquid and season well with salt and pepper.
5. Simmer over low heat, stirring well, for 15 minutes. Serve hot.

## Ful Medames

These are small brown beans which are particularly popular in Egypt when made into this unusual dish with hard-boiled eggs.

*1lb (450g) Egyptian brown beans*
*2 garlic cloves*
*2 tbsps chopped fresh parsley*
*4 hard-boiled eggs*
*salt and pepper*
*olive oil*
*lemon quarters*

1. Soak the beans in cold water overnight. Drain well and cover with fresh cold water. Bring slowly to boiling point, then simmer for about 1¼ hours until the beans are tender. Drain well.
2. Crush the garlic and stir into the beans. Sprinkle with parsley.
3. Top each portion with an egg. Hand salt, pepper, oil and lemon quarters separately, so that each person seasons his own portion.

## Pease Pudding

A traditional accompaniment to boiled pork, ham or beef, or to roast pork. The mixture may be boiled or baked.

*1lb (450g) split peas*
*salt and pepper*
*2oz (50g) butter or dripping*
*2 eggs*

1. Soak the peas in cold water overnight. Drain well, cover in cold water and bring to the boil. Cover and simmer for 2 hours until the peas are very soft. Drain well.
2. Mash the peas and season well. Mix with the butter or dripping and beat in the eggs.
3. Put into a greased pudding basin, cover and simmer for 1 hour. Turn out, slice and serve.
4. If preferred, put the mixture into a greased pie dish and bake at 180°C (350°F), gas mark 4 for 30 minutes.

## Mushroom and Broad Bean Salad

If broad beans are not available, kidney or haricot beans may be used, but will need soaking and longer cooking.

*6oz (150g) broad beans*
*8oz (225g) button mushrooms*
*4 spring onions*
*¼ pint (150ml) natural yoghurt*
*salt and pepper*

1. Cook the beans in salted water until just tender. Drain and leave until cold.
2. Wipe the mushrooms and leave whole.
3. Chop the onions finely.
4. Mix the beans, mushrooms and onions with the yoghurt and season to taste with salt and pepper.

## Kidney Bean Salad

A 'hot' and colourful salad which may be served as a first course or used as an accompaniment to meat or fish. It also makes a good filling for pitta bread.

*8oz (225g) red kidney beans*
*1 small cauliflower*
*1 green pepper*
*2 celery sticks*
*1 small onion*
*2 tbsps chopped fresh parsley*
*6 tbsps oil*
*3 tbsps wine vinegar*
*Tabasco sauce*

1. Soak the beans in cold water overnight. Drain well, rinse in cold water and drain. Cover with fresh water and bring to the boil. Boil for 10 minutes, cover and simmer for 1 hour. Drain well and cool.
2. Put the beans into a serving bowl. Add the cauliflower divided into small florets.
3. Core and seed the pepper and cut the flesh in strips. Slice the celery thinly and chop the onion very finely. Mix the pepper, celery and onion into the beans. Sprinkle with parsley.
4. Mix the oil and vinegar and season well with Tabasco sauce. Pour over the salad. Leave to stand for 2 hours and serve cold.

## Italian Bean and Tuna Salad

An excellent summer dish which may be a main course or can be served in small portions as a first course.

*12oz (350g) cannellini beans*
*12oz (350g) flageolet beans*
*7oz (200g) can tuna fish in brine*
*salt and pepper*
*lettuce or chicory leaves*
*6 tbsps olive oil*
*2 tbsps lemon juice*
*1 small onion*
*12 black olives*
*1 tbsp chopped fresh parsley*
*1 tbsp chopped fresh marjoram*

1. Soak the beans separately in cold water overnight. Drain well and rinse in cold water. Drain, and put the beans into a large pan. Cover with cold water, bring to the boil and boil for 10 minutes. Cover and simmer for 1 hour until cooked but unbroken.
2. Drain the beans well and leave until just cold. Drain the tuna and break into small chunks. Mix with the beans and season well with salt and pepper.
3. Arrange lettuce and chicory leaves on a serving dish and pile the bean mixture in the centre.
4. Mix the oil and lemon juice and pour over the beans.
5. Garnish with thinly sliced onion rings, olives, parsley and marjoram. Chill for 30 minutes and serve.

## Lentil Salad

It is worth cooking an extra supply of lentils when preparing other dishes, so that leftovers may be used for this unusual salad.

*2 tbsps vegetable oil*
*1 large onion*
*1 garlic clove*
*1 bay leaf*
*8oz (225g) lentils*
*2 tomatoes*
*1 green pepper*
*4 tbsps olive oil*
*2 tbsps lemon juice*
*½ tsp mustard powder*
*½ tsp sugar*
*salt and pepper*
*2 tbsps chopped fresh parsley*

1. Heat the oil and cook the finely chopped onion and crushed garlic until soft and golden.
2. Add the bay leaf and lentils, and pour on water to cover. Bring to the boil, cover and simmer for 40 minutes until the lentils are tender. Drain well and discard the bay leaf. Leave the lentils to stand for 5 minutes.
3. Skin the tomatoes, discard seeds and cut the flesh into small pieces. Fold into the lentils and put into a serving bowl.
4. Discard the seeds and membranes from the pepper and dice the flesh. Stir into the lentil mixture.
5. Mix the olive oil, lemon juice, mustard, sugar and plenty of salt and pepper. Pour over the warm lentils.
6. Cool and then chill for 30 minutes. Sprinkle with parsley and serve.

## Black-Eye Seafood Salad

This is a particularly delicious dish served chilled for a summer meal, but it can also be a refreshing first course.

*4oz (100g) black-eye beans*
*8oz (225g) white fish (haddock or cod)*
*7oz (200g) canned tuna in brine*
*4oz (100g) peeled prawns*
*1 small onion*
*6 tbsps oil*
*3 tbsps wine vinegar*
*juice of ½ lemon*
*2 tbsps tomato purée*
*1 tsp grated lemon rind*
*Tabasco sauce*
*salt and pepper*
*1 tbsp chopped fresh parsley*

1. Soak the beans overnight in cold water. Drain well, rinse and drain. Cover with fresh water, bring to the boil and boil for 10 minutes. Cover and simmer for 40 minutes. Drain well.
2. Poach the fish in a little salted water until just cooked. Drain, skin and break into flakes.
3. Drain the tuna and break into flakes. Mix the white fish, tuna and prawns with the beans.
4. Mix the oil, vinegar, lemon juice, tomato purée, lemon rind, Tabasco, salt and pepper to taste. Pour over the salad and toss lightly.
5. Leave to stand for 1 hour. Sprinkle with parsley and serve cold.

# SPROUTING GRAINS, BEANS AND PULSES

Many cereal grains, beans and pulses may be sprouted to provide food which is rich in essential protein and vitamins. Sprouts are very easily digested and make quick flavoursome additions to meals. Mung (Chinese) bean sprouts are widely available fresh and canned, but all types of sprouts are very easily grown at home.

It is important only to use seeds specially sold for sprouting, which must be free from chemicals and certified as edible (some garden seeds are treated to make them easy to grow and free from pests). Grains, beans and pulses purchased for eating from grocers or health food shops are of course safe to eat, but if they are cracked, broken or old, they will not sprout successfully.

Sprouts are harvested when they are between 3-5 days old, as they soon lose flavour and food value. They will keep crisp for a week in the salad compartment of a refrigerator. Sprouts may be eaten raw, or lightly steamed, or simmered in water or stock for 4 minutes, or lightly stir-fried in a little oil, but they must always be slightly crisp to eat. They may be used in salads, or mixed with cooked vegetables, or form part of a stuffing for vegetables. They may also be included in baked goods, or may be blended into health-giving drinks with yoghurt, fruit and vegetables.

The recipes in this section are for sprouts grown from readily available seeds, but different types of sprouts may be substituted.

## Easy Sprouting Method

Special seed sprouters are available, but for early experiments, jam jars are perfectly adequate, clean and easy to use. Some pieces of muslin or cheesecloth are also needed. Four level teaspoons of seed equal approximately ½oz (15g) and these will convert into 5-8oz (125-225g) food.

Wash a jam jar thoroughly and cut a piece of muslin that will fit comfortably over the opening. Put in 4 teaspoons seed and cover with the muslin, securing with an elastic band or piece of string. Fill with tepid water through the lid and shake well to clean the seed. Drain and repeat the process 3 times.

Put the jar on its side where a reasonable temperature 17-21°C (60-70°F) can be maintained. Every morning and evening, fill the jar with cold or tepid water and drain it off. Harvest the seeds after 3-4 days, and rinse well before using.

Sprouts grown in the dark will be white, and beans have a better flavour if grown in this way. Leafy sprouts such as alfalfa are better grown in the light so that they remain green. White sprouts may be 'greened' by leaving them in light or indirect sunlight for a few hours.

The individual growing instructions which follow are for those seeds most relevant to the subject of this book.

*Aduki beans* are a rich source of protein, essential amino acids, lysine, iron, niacin and calcium. Sprout at 22°C (72°F), rinsing 4 times daily. Harvest at 1in (2.5cm) length, after about 4 days.

*Alfalfa* is a rich source of protein, amino acids, minerals and vitamins. Sprout at 22°C (72°F), rinsing twice daily. Harvest at 1½-2in (3.75-5cm) length, after 3-5 days.

*Barley* should be sprouted at 21-27°C (70-80°F), rinsing twice daily. Harvest when root is length of seed, after 3-4 days.

*Beans* of all kinds are a rich source of protein, iron, phosphorus, potassium, vitamins and calcium. Sprout at 20-30°C (68-86°F), rinsing 3-4 times daily. Harvest at 1-2in (2.5-5cm) length, after 3-5 days.

*Chick Peas* are a good source of protein and iron and have trace quantities of vitamins A and C which are increased by sprouting. Sprout at 20-22°C (68-72°F), rinsing 4-5 times daily. Harvest when root is ½in (1.25cm) length, after 3 days.

*Fenugreek* is rich in protein, iron and vitamin A and has a spicy flavour. Sprout at 20-30°C (68-86°F), rinsing twice daily. Harvest at 3in (7.5cm) length, after 4-5 days.

*Lentils* are rich in protein, with substantial amounts of vitamin B, iron and phosphorus, and traces of vitamins C and E are increased when sprouted. Sprout at 20-30°C (68-86°F), rinsing twice daily. Harvest at 1in (2.5cm), after 3-4 days.

*Maize (sweetcorn)* sprouts have a sweet flavour. Sprout at 22-30°C (72-86°F), rinsing twice daily. Harvest when root is ½in (1.25cm) long, after 2-3 days.

*Millet* is rich in iron and niacin and is a source of protein, phosphorus and vitamin $B_2$. The flavour is sweet and the grain easily digested. Sprout at 21-27°C (70-80°F), rinsing twice daily. Harvest when root is ¼in (0.75cm) long, after 3-4 days.

*Mung (Chinese) beans* are a good source of choline and vitamin E, both of which increase during sprouting. Sprout at 20-30°C (68-86°F), rinsing 3-4 times daily. Harvest at 2in (5cm) length, after 3-4 days.

*Oats* contain protein and all essential amino acids and are rich in vitamin C. They tend to sour quickly and need little water for sprouting. Sprout at 21-27°C (70-80°F), rinsing just enough to keep seeds moist. Harvest when the leading root (the longest of the three) is the same length as the oat grain, after 3-4 days.

*Peas* are rich in protein and contain all the essential amino acids. Sprout at 10-20°C (50-68°F), rinsing twice daily. Harvest when root is length of seed, after 3 days.

*Rice* of all types may be sprouted and brown rice is best. It is a good source of niacin and some vitamin E. Sprouting increases vitamin C. Sprout at 10-27°C (50-80°F) rinsing twice daily. Harvest when root is length of grain, after 3-4 days.

*Rye* has some protein and is rich in manganese, phosphorus, potassium and iron. Sprout at 10-20°C (50-68°F), rinsing twice daily. Harvest when root is length of grain, after 3-4 days.

*Soya beans* are rich in protein, vitamin B and lecithin. They ferment easily and may be difficult to sprout in hot weather, and must be flooded several times daily with lukewarm water, then drained. Sprout only fresh seeds at 20-30°C (68-86°F), rinsing every 3 hours. Harvest at 2in (5cm) length, after 4 days.

*Triticale* is a cross between wheat and rye and contains more protein than any other cereal grain, as well as essential amino acids. Sprout at 20-30°C (68-86°F), rinsing twice daily. Harvest when roots are ¼in (0.75cm) long, after 2-3 days.

*Wheat* is rich in vitamin E. Its low vitamin C content is increased six times over when sprouted. Sprout at 21-27°C (70-80°F), rinsing twice daily. Harvest when roots are ½in (1.25cm) long, after 3-4 days.

# SPROUTING GRAINS, BEANS AND PULSES

## Bean Sprout and Corn Soup

A delicious soup with plenty of texture which is almost a complete meal if served with wholemeal bread.

*1 small onion*
*2 celery sticks*
*2 medium potatoes*
*1¼ pints (750ml) chicken stock*
*1 tbsp lemon juice*
*salt and pepper*
*8oz (225g) cooked chicken*
*4oz (100g) Mung (Chinese) bean sprouts*
*4oz (100g) corn kernels*
*¾ pint (450ml) creamy milk*
*2 tbsps chopped fresh parsley or chives*

1. Chop the onion and celery finely. Dice the potatoes.
2. Cook the onion and celery with the butter over low heat until the vegetables are soft and golden. Add the potatoes and continue cooking over low heat, stirring well, for 5 minutes.
3. Add the stock, lemon juice, salt and pepper and bring to the boil. Cover and simmer for 10 minutes.
4. Dice the chicken and add to the soup with the bean sprouts and corn kernels. Add to the soup and simmer for 15 minutes.
5. Stir in the milk, reheat and serve hot sprinkled with parsley.

## Fenugreek and Potato Soup

A quickly made soup with a spicy flavour which is suitable for summer or winter meals.

*8oz (225g) potatoes*
*¾ pint (450ml) chicken stock or water*
*8oz (225g) fenugreek sprouts*
*¼ pint (150ml) creamy milk*
*salt and pepper*

1. Boil the potatoes in the stock or water until tender. Lift out the potatoes and reserve the cooking liquid.
2. Put the potatoes into a liquidizer or food processor with three-quarters of the sprouts and the milk, and blend until smooth.
3. Return to the saucepan with the cooking liquid. Bring to boiling point and simmer for 3 minutes.
4. Season to taste and garnish with remaining fenugreek sprouts.

## Crunchy Chinese Salad

A particularly good winter salad which is colourful and refreshing.

*8oz (225g) Mung (Chinese) bean sprouts*
*1 large carrot*
*2 celery sticks*
*2oz (50g) cashew nuts or peanuts*
*1 tbsp sesame seeds*
*2 tbsps oil*
*1 tbsp wine vinegar*
*watercress, lettuce or chicory*

1. Put the bean sprouts into a serving bowl.
2. Grate the carrot coarsely. Chop the celery finely.
3. Mix the carrot and celery into the bean sprouts and stir in the nuts and sesame seeds.
4. Mix the oil and vinegar, pour over the salad and toss well.
5. Serve on a bed of watercress, lettuce or chicory.

## Raw Energy Salad

A salad made in a couple of minutes which is full of good fresh flavours and crunchy textures.

*6oz (150g) button mushrooms*
*4oz (100g) Mung (Chinese) bean sprouts*
*4oz (100g) alfalfa sprouts*
*3oz (75g) shelled peas*
*4 tbsps oil*
*2 tbsps lemon juice*
*1 garlic clove*

1. Wipe the mushrooms but do not peel them. Slice thinly and put into a serving bowl.
2. Stir in the bean sprouts and alfalfa sprouts and the uncooked peas.
3. Mix together the oil, lemon juice and crushed garlic and pour over the salad. Toss well and serve at once.

## Green Soup

An unusual chilled summer soup, similar to the Spanish *gaspacho* which makes the best of alfalfa sprouts.

*6 green tomatoes*
*1 medium green pepper*
*1 small cucumber*
*1 garlic clove*
*4 tbsps olive oil*
*2 tbsps white wine vinegar*
*pinch of salt*
*pinch of ground cumin*
*8oz (225g) alfalfa sprouts*
*2 spring onions*
*¼ pint (150ml) dry white wine*
*3 tbsps iced water*

1. Skin the tomatoes and chop them roughly. Mince the tomatoes, green pepper and unpeeled cucumber, or chop them finely in a food processor.
2. Mix the vegetables with crushed garlic, oil, vinegar, salt and cumin.
3. Chop the alfalfa sprouts and spring onions and mix into the tomato mixture. Chill for 2 hours.
4. Just before serving, stir in the wine and iced water.
5. If liked, garnish with some chopped fresh herbs, or small cubes of toasted bread.

# Summer Beans and Sprouts

An original way of serving young French beans to make them into a very special vegetable dish, particularly good with chicken or fish.

*1lb (450g) French beans*
*2oz (50g) butter*
*1 tbsp oil*
*1 small onion or 4 spring onions*
*4oz (100g) Mung (Chinese) bean sprouts*
*2 tbsps chopped fresh parsley*
*pinch of ground nutmeg*
*salt and pepper*

1. Cook the whole beans in boiling salted water until tender. Drain well.
2. Heat the butter and oil and cook the finely chopped onion or spring onions over low heat until soft and golden.
3. Add the bean sprouts and stir quickly.
4. Add the cooked beans and toss until the beans are hot.
5. Sprinkle with parsley, nutmeg, salt and pepper and put into a warm serving dish.

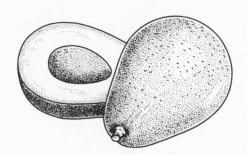

# Whole Earth Salad

A whole-meal salad which is surprisingly filling. Serve it with crusty French bread or wholemeal bread.

*4oz (100g) Mung (Chinese) bean sprouts*
*4oz (100g) aduki bean sprouts*
*4oz (100g) alfalfa sprouts*
*4oz (100g) Cheddar cheese*
*1 cabbage lettuce*
*1 green pepper*
*3 spring onions*
*2 tbsps chopped fresh parsley*
*4 tomatoes*
*1 avocado*
*3 tbsps lemon juice*
*6 tbsps oil*

1. Mix the three types of sprouts in a salad bowl.
2. Cut the cheese into small cubes and add to the sprouts.
3. Shred the lettuce and chop the green pepper and onions finely. Add to the bowl with the parsley.
4. Skin the tomatoes and deseed them. Chop the flesh roughly and add to the bowl.
5. Peel the avocado and dice the flesh. Put into the lemon juice and leave to stand for 1 minute.
6. Add the oil and pour the dressing over the salad. Toss well and serve at once.

## Green Rice Salad

A subtle blend of herb and spice flavours enhances this
attractive looking salad. It may be made with brown rice,
but this takes about 40 minutes to cook.

*3oz (75g) long-grain rice*
*1 bunch watercress*
*4oz (100g) fenugreek sprouts*
*2 tbsps chopped fresh parsley*
*2 tbsps chopped fresh chives*
*salt and pepper*
*4 tbsps salad oil*
*2 tbsps wine vinegar*

1. Cook the rice in boiling salted water for 12 minutes
   until tender. Drain well and rinse in cold water. Drain
   thoroughly and put into a serving bowl. Leave until
   cold.
2. Trim the lower stems of the watercress and chop the
   leaves and upper stalks roughly. Stir into the rice with
   the fenugreek sprouts, parsley, chives, salt and
   pepper.
3. Just before serving, mix the oil and vinegar, pour over
   the salad and toss well.

## Sprout-Stuffed Tomatoes

These make an attractive first course or an
accompaniment to other dishes in a buffet meal. Large
Beefeater or Marmande tomatoes are the best to use.

*4 large tomatoes*
*2oz (50g) Mung (Chinese) bean sprouts*
*2oz (50g) alfalfa sprouts*
*1 tbsp chopped fresh chives*
*2 tbsps oil*
*1 tbsp lemon juice*
*salt and pepper*

1. Remove the stalks from the tomatoes. Turn them
   upside down and cut off a 'lid' from the bottom of each
   tomato. Scoop out the seeds and discard.
2. Scoop out most of the tomato flesh and put through a
   sieve.
3. Chop the bean sprouts and alfalfa sprouts and mix
   with the tomato flesh, chives, oil, lemon juice and
   plenty of salt and pepper.
4. Fill the tomato cases and replace the lids. Chill before
   serving.

## Baked Fish with Bean Sprouts

Bean sprouts make a pleasant contrast to the soft fish in this quickly-assembled dish.

*4oz (100g) Mung (Chinese) bean sprouts*
*2 tbsps chopped fresh parsley*
*1 tbsp chopped fresh chives*
*2 tsps chopped fresh dill*
*1lb (450g) cod or haddock fillet*
*2oz (50g) butter*
*1 tbsp lemon juice*
*salt and pepper*

1. Grease an ovenware dish. Mix the sprouts and herbs and sprinkle over the base of the dish.
2. Cut the fish into 4 pieces and arrange on the sprouts.
3. Cut the butter into small flakes and dot over the fish. Sprinkle with lemon juice and season well with salt and pepper.
4. Bake at 200°C (400°F), gas mark 6 for 25 minutes.

## New Potatoes with Bean Sprout Sauce

This makes a light summer meal on its own, or can be an accompaniment to meat, poultry or fish.

*1½lb (675g) new potatoes*
*4oz (100g) butter*
*1 garlic clove*
*8oz (225g) mushrooms*
*4oz (100g) Mung (Chinese) bean sprouts*
*2 tbsps chopped fresh parsley*
*2 tbsps chopped fresh chives*
*salt and pepper*

1. Scrub the potatoes and cook with or without skins until tender.
2. Melt the butter and cook the crushed garlic for 1 minute. Add sliced mushrooms and stir over low heat for 5 minutes.
3. Stir in the bean sprouts and cook for 1 minute.
4. Stir in the parsley and chives, and season well with salt and pepper.
5. Pour over the potatoes and serve at once.

## Fenugreek Dip

A refreshingly flavoured dip to serve as a first course or at a drinks party.

*4oz (100g) cottage cheese*
*¼ pint (150ml) natural yoghurt*
*4oz (100g) fenugreek sprouts*
*1 garlic clove*
*pinch of caraway seeds*
*salt*

1. Sieve the cottage cheese and mix with the yoghurt until smooth.
2. Chop the fenugreek finely. Crush the garlic clove.
3. Mix all the ingredients and season well with salt.
4. Put into a serving bowl and chill for 2 hours.
5. Put the bowl on a large dish or tray and surround with crisps, pieces of celery, cucumber and carrots.

## Cream Cheese and Fenugreek Log

This log may be served on a cheese board, or may be sliced and placed on biscuits or rounds of wholemeal bread.

*8oz (225g) cream cheese*
*2oz (50g) fenugreek sprouts*
*½ tsp made mustard*
*salt and pepper*
*2 tbsps chopped fresh parsley*
*2 tbsps chopped fresh chives*
*2 tbsps thyme*

1. Mix the cheese with finely chopped fenugreek sprouts and season with mustard, salt and pepper.
2. Shape into a cylinder and chill for 15 minutes.
3. Mix the chopped herbs on a flat surface and roll the 'log' in the herb mixture until well coated.
4. Chill for at least 1 hour before serving.

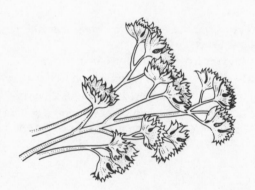

## Mushroom and Bean Sprout Spread

A richly flavoured mixture which is suitable for a light lunch or supper if served on rounds of wholemeal toast.

*8oz (225g) mushrooms*
*2oz (50g) butter*
*4oz (100g) Mung (Chinese) bean sprouts or aduki bean sprouts*
*1 tbsp chopped fresh parsley*
*1 tbsp chopped fresh chives*
*1 level tbsp cornflour*
*2 tbsps water*
*pinch of salt*

1. Chop the mushrooms and cook in butter over low heat for 5 minutes until soft.
2. Chop the bean sprouts finely and stir into the butter with the herbs.
3. Mix the cornflour and water and stir into the pan. Season well with salt.
4. Simmer for 3 minutes until the mixture is thick. Serve at once.

## Fenugreek Potatoes

A delicious way of preparing the ever-popular fried potatoes with a slightly spicy flavour.

*1lb (450g) cooked potatoes*
*3 tbsps oil*
*½ tsp turmeric*
*8oz (225g) fenugreek sprouts*
*pinch of cayenne pepper*
*pinch of salt*

1. Chop the potatoes. Heat the oil in a thick frying pan and add the potatoes and turmeric. Cook for 5 minutes, stirring and lifting them often as they change colour.
2. Add the fenugreek sprouts, cayenne pepper and salt. Put on a lid and continue cooking for 5 minutes.

## Triticale Pancakes

Serve these puffy little pancakes with a crisp salad, and with some grilled bacon if liked.

2oz (50g) coarse oatmeal
6 tbsps water
2oz (50g) wholemeal flour
1 tsp baking powder
pinch of salt
4oz (100g) aduki bean sprouts
2oz (50g) triticale sprouts
1 small onion
2 eggs
1oz (25g) melted butter
oil for frying

1. Soak the oatmeal in the water for 1 hour.
2. Mix in the flour, baking powder and salt.
3. Chop the sprouts finely and chop the onion very finely.
4. Add to the mixture with beaten eggs and butter. Beat well.
5. Heat oil in a thick frying pan and drop in spoonfuls of the mixture. Flatten slightly with the back of a spoon. Cook until golden brown on all sides. Serve hot.

## Alfalfa Biscuits

Tempting little biscuits with an unusual texture.

3oz (75g) clear honey
2oz (50g) butter
few drops of vanilla essence
2oz (50g) wholemeal flour
¼ tsp baking powder
¼ tsp bicarbonate of soda
4oz (100g) rolled oats
2oz (50g) alfalfa sprouts

1. Preheat oven to 180°C (350°F), gas mark 4. Grease 3 baking sheets.
2. Cream the honey, butter and essence until light and fluffy.
3. Work in the flour, baking powder and soda.
4. Add the oats and chopped sprouts and mix well.
5. Drop spoonfuls on baking sheets. Bake for 12 minutes.
6. Lift carefully on to a wire rack to cool.

# Date and Triticale Teabread

Serve this teabread freshly baked, sliced and spread with butter or margarine and honey if liked. It is also very good spread with cream cheese.

*3oz (75g) stoned dates*
*7 tbsps boiling water*
*4oz (100g) light soft brown sugar*
*1 tbsp melted butter*
*1 egg*
*6oz (150g) wholemeal flour*
*1 tsps bicarbonate of soda*
*½ tsp baking powder*
*pinch of salt*
*2oz (50g) chopped walnuts*
*1oz (25g) triticale sprouts*

1. Preheat oven to 180°C (350°F), gas mark 4. Grease and base-line a 1lb (450g) loaf tin.
2. Chop the dates and pour on boiling water. Leave to stand for 30 minutes.
3. Stir together the sugar, butter and egg.
4. Mix the flour, soda, baking powder and salt. Work in the egg mixture with the dates and water.
5. Add the walnuts and finely chopped triticale sprouts. Mix thoroughly and put into the prepared tin.
6. Bake for 45 minutes. Leave in the tin for 5 minutes, and then turn on to a wire rack to cool.

# Alfalfa Honey Cakes

Small cakes with a crunchy texture which are good with milk or a hot drink.

*8oz (225g) wholemeal flour*
*2oz (50g) demerara sugar*
*1½ tsp baking powder*
*pinch of ground cinnamon*
*pinch of salt*
*2oz (50g) clear honey*
*1 egg*
*12 tbsps milk*
*2oz (50g) melted butter*
*2oz (50g) alfalfa sprouts*
*2oz (50g) chopped walnuts*

1. Preheat oven to 200°C (400°F), gas mark 6. Grease 24 individual cake tins.
2. Stir together flour, sugar, baking powder, cinnamon and salt.
3. Beat together the honey, egg, milk and butter and beat into the dry ingredients.
4. Chop the alfalfa sprouts and add to the mixture with the walnuts.
5. Divide the mixture between the cake tins, and bake for 20 minutes.
6. Cool on a wire rack.

# INDEX